KILLER WOMEN
OF MICHIGAN

KILLER WOMEN
OF MICHIGAN

TOBIN T. BUHK

THE
History
PRESS

Published by The History Press
Charleston, SC
www.historypress.com

First published 2024

Manufactured in the United States

ISBN 9781467156202

Library of Congress Control Number: 2023947094

CONTENTS

Introduction   7

1. Rogues Gallery (1866–1925)   11
2. A Day in the Life (June 12–13, 1900)   33
3. Taken for a Ride (Benton Harbor, 1924)   37
4. For Services Rendered (Niles, 1928)   47
5. The "Baby Murder Farm" Case (Eau Claire, 1929)   59
6. The Heiress and the Mechanic (Flint, 1932)   75
7. All in the Family (Cheboygan, 1932)   85
8. Chemical Divorce (Baraga, 1932)   93
9. Three Sirens (Detroit, 1935)   97
10. You Belong to Me: Murder of the Love Slave (Ann Arbor, 1936)   115
11. Housden, We Have a Problem (Detroit, 1944)   123
12. The Housewife and the Orphan (Williamston, 1947)   131
13. The Bark Is Worse Than the Bite (Pontiac, 1984)   141
14. Twisted Fairy Tale (Royal Oak, 1984)   147
15. Bad Things Happen in Threes (Wayland, 1990)   151

Notes   157
Bibliography   171
About the Author   175

INTRODUCTION

The Cases: The Mad, the Bad, and the Sad

Want to see a black widow? Check out "A Rogues Gallery." Serial killers your thing? See "Bad Things Happen in Threes." Fascinated by crime passionnel? Try "The Heiress and the Mechanic." Interested in love triangles? Check out "Taken for a Ride" or "All in the Family." Cold-blooded murder for profit? Yep. Turn to "Three Sirens" or "Twisted Fairy Tale."

They're all here: Florence, Deetie, Oakel, Helen, Elizabeth, Nina, Diane, Carol and many, many others. The ultimate lineup of the women who committed the "Big M" in Michigan.

Who's In, Who's Out

This book is not an encyclopedic study of Michigan's female offenders. True-crime aficionados will no doubt wonder why the crime of (fill in the blank) is missing. More than likely, this omission stems from a desire to avoid cases that have been covered extensively by other authors, including yours truly. Any discussion of Michigan's most dangerous female offenders, for example, would need to include Mary Murphy McKnight, but an exhaustive treatment of this case appears in *Michigan's Strychnine Saint*.

NOT HOW BUT WHY: A QUESTION OF MOTIVE

Be it garroting, bludgeoning, shooting, stabbing or poisoning, there are only so many ways to dispatch an unwanted husband, tiresome lover or troublesome rival. When it comes to a study of crime, the "how"—which often leaves walls spattered with cast-off stains and carpets saturated with blood—can attract attention the same way as a gaper's block on the highway. The morbidly curious, eager to catch a glimpse of carnage, slow down as they pass the immediate aftermath of a high-speed collision. Likewise, some find blood-drenched crime scenes oddly fascinating, but as interesting as investigating the "how" can be, delving into the "why" is an infinitely more complex undertaking. It lives somewhere deep inside the psyche of those who commit murder.

The posterchild for the "why" behind crimes committed by women wasn't entirely a real person. Ever since Shakespeare's iconic character Lady MacBeth uttered her immortal line "Out damned spot," she became a symbol for the psychology behind criminal behavior. Her behavior helped bring the "why" behind criminal acts, particularly those perpetrated by women, to the forefront and would provide models for what would centuries later become the field of criminal psychology.

Lady MacBeth does not make an appearance in the following pages, at least not physically. She might have a spiritual parallel in Josephine Upton, who channeled the infamous Lady MacBeth by egging on young Dickie Gorman to slay the king, played by Upton's allegedly wicked husband Frank. And like her semi-fictitious forerunner, Josephine Upton provides an interesting psychological case study of how and why women conspire to commit murder.

Josephine Upton's sisters in crime and cohabitants in this volume likewise provide excellent fodder for the student of criminal psychology who wants to explore the "why."

RELEVANCE OF OLD (IN SOME CASES REALLY, OLD) CRIMES

George Santayana famously noted, "Those who cannot remember the past are condemned to repeat it." The yellowed pages of yesteryears' newspapers and the dust-covered boxes of age-old court files contain stories that are eerily similar to crimes of the present. Shining a light on these crimes can help illuminate the how and why of today's crimes and might even represent cautionary tales for the future.

Consider the case of Amanda Simons, who drowned her three stepchildren in the Kalamazoo River. The apparently motiveless crime led to a life imprisonment in 1869. Some 121 years later, Diane Spencer admitted to smothering three of her infant children. Like Simons, she offered no motive other than that she felt a need to kill. Simons's case barely survived into historical record, but a close examination of the scant documentation might reveal some interesting parallels between her story and Spencer's.

To meet the killer women of Michigan, turn the page.

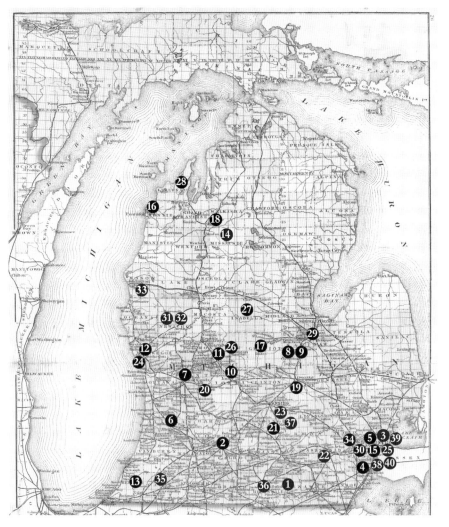

Murder map of Michigan showing the locations of crimes committed by Michigan's most dangerous women, 1866–1925. *Original map from the Library of Congress.*

1
ROGUES GALLERY
1866-1925

They are the mad, the bad and the sad.

During the seven decades from the end of the Civil War until the mid-1920s, female offenders serving long-term sentences were housed at the old Detroit House of Correction—a multifaceted prison population that also included local short-timers of both sexes and (during the prison's first few decades) prisoners from the federal territories. In this time span, a total of thirty-four women from around the state were sentenced to life.

The following case summaries include all thirty-four lifers along with a few dishonorable mentions.

1. Arvella Smith, Lenawee, Life (1866, pardoned in 1878)

Sixty-six-year-old widower Aaron Smith lived with his thirteen-year-old daughter, Josephine; his twenty-two-year-old son, John; and John's wife, Arvella (who according to one source was "a confirmed prostitute"), in the small community of Hudson. Josephine became enamored of a male acquaintance of Arvella's, and the two couples rented a cottage on Round Lake. Shortly after, Josephine learned that she was pregnant. Arvella convinced the girl that her father would never let her marry and needled her into serving the old man arsenic-laced tea. When Aaron became suddenly ill, the attending physician suspected heavy metal poisoning, which prompted Arvella to scribble a note asking Josephine to stop giving her father "the

Black and white prisoners stand shoulder to shoulder in this rare image of female inmates of the Detroit House of Correction, circa 1899. At the time, the prison was one of the only penal facilities in America not to practice racial segregation. Note the prisoner standing fourth from the right. She's making a provocative gesture to the cameraman. *Library of Congress.*

tea." After the note was intercepted, John and Arvella fled. Overcome with remorse, John attempted to poison himself but survived to face the music in court. Josephine turned state's evidence, her testimony sending both John and Arvella to prison for life. Arvella Smith was pardoned in 1878.[1]

2. Sarah Haviland, Calhoun, Life (1866, pardoned in 1896)

Thirty-eight-year-old Sarah Haviland poisoned her three children so she would be free to marry Daniel J. Baker. Sentenced to life, Haviland became housekeeper for a succession of wardens at the state prison in Jackson. Known for a gentle and kind demeanor, the woman who murdered her children for love became a beloved figure in the warden's residence, earning her the nickname "Aunt" Haviland among the children who grew up there. When the female prisoners were moved to the Detroit House of Correction in the 1870s, Haviland remained behind. After serving thirty years, prisoner No. 20 was granted an unconditional pardon by Governor John T. Rich in 1896 and left prison at the age of sixty-eight.

3. Virginia Doyle, Wayne, Twenty Years (1870, died in prison in 1878)

Eating food and drink prepared by Virginia Doyle was a potentially fatal proposition. Her first husband died after a bout of burning stomach pain. History repeated itself for Doyle's second husband, who also died after crippling stomach pain twisted him into knots. In 1870, the thirty-seven-year-old Michigan Borgia attempted to dispatch her live-in mother, Catherine de Baptiste, by spiking pudding, a baked apple and a glass of wine with arsenic. These unsuccessful attempts landed Doyle in prison for twenty years. Her sentence ended early in May 1878 when she died inside the Detroit House of Correction.

4. Elizabeth Newington, Wayne, Acquitted

When eight-year-old Amza Newington died after suffering from severe stomach spasms, residents of Flat Rock began to gossip about a wicked stepmother who had purchased strychnine in the days before the boy's death. A postmortem revealed traces of the heavy metal poison, which put Elizabeth Newington on trial for murder in 1883. Newington, described by a *Free Press* reporter as "large, masculine-looking woman of apparently 50 years of age," admitted purchasing strychnine to silence the incessant barking of a neighbor's dog but insisted the poison did not end up in her beloved stepson's food.[2] Although she was convicted in the Flat Rock court of public opinion, the jury freed Newington with a verdict of "not guilty."

5. Rosa Schweistahl, Wayne, Life (1869, died in prison in 1885)

Fifty-six-year-old Rosa Schneider (née Rothmann) fell head-over-heels in love with Nicholas Schweistahl, so it came as no surprise that the death of

The Detroit House of Correction: the destination for all female lifers, 1860–1925. *Library of Congress*.

her brother Henry a few days before the wedding did not deter her from walking down the aisle. The marriage went without a hitch, but when authorities discovered that Rosa's supposed brother was really her husband and found a large amount of arsenic in her possession—which Rosa said she acquired for the purpose of killing rats—she was tried for and convicted of murder. In a written confession, Rosa explained that she had plotted to poison her husband because he spent all of their money on "lager." Older than most of her fellow inmates in the Detroit House of Correction, Rosa became a beloved, mother-like figure. Dubbed "Mother of the House," she died on Christmas Day 1885.[3]

6. Amanda Simons, Allegan, Life (1869, died in prison in 1877)

Eighteen-year-old Amanda Simons committed what many considered the worst crime in Allegan County history when she led her three stepchildren down to the edge of the Kalamazoo River and drowned them in two and a half feet of water. Married just three months earlier to Frank Simons, Amanda admitted to murdering her husband's children: ten-year-old Joseph, eight-year-old John and three-year-old Stella. She did not supply a motive but attempted to deflect some of the blame by explaining, in the words of an *Allegan Journal* writer, that "another colored woman advised her to commit the deed."[4] Amanda Simons appeared detached when the judge sentenced her to life in prison. According to a journalist in the gallery, she "maintained a look of stolid indifference, seeming to care but little whether the sentence was for one year or for life."[5] Simons's life sentence ended after three years when she died in prison at the age of twenty-six.

7. Esther Coffeen, Kent, Life (1877, pardoned in 1882)

On a cold September midnight in 1877, Coffeen set fire to a Grand Rapids tenement building owned by John Giddings. No one perished in the fire, which caused only minor damage to the building amounting to about $300. Nonetheless, Coffeen received a life sentence at hard labor in the state prison at Jackson. After her conviction, Coffeen became a pawn in a legal battle. The warden of the state prison at Jackson refused to admit her on the grounds that female prisoners were supposed to serve time in the Detroit House of Correction, but the sentencing judge likewise refused to amend the sentence. Coffeen spent the next two years confined to the Jackson County Jail. In 1879, the Michigan legislature settled the debate with a law requiring female inmates to serve their time in Detroit, and Coffeen was transferred to the Detroit House of Correction. By the time of her transfer, she was dying of cancer, which left her a hideous sight, prompting one reporter to note, "A portion of her face had been slowly eaten away." She was pardoned in 1882.[6]

8. Mary Jane Smith, Saginaw, Fifteen Years (1876, died in prison in 1880)

Wife of a Chesaning farmer, Mary Jane Smith began an affair with farmhand Norris "Nock" Alexander. With the assistance of her sister Julia and her sister's husband, Freeman Cargin, they plotted the farmer's demise, which occurred when Freeman Cargin bludgeoned Charles Smith to death while he slept. The trio then took the body to the barn and set it on fire. Both Alexander and Mary Jane Smith turned state's evidence and testified against the principals. For his cooperation, Alexander received a sentence of ten years. Convicted as an accessory, Mary Jane Smith was sentenced to fifteen years; Julia and Freeman Cargin each received life. Both sisters served time in the Detroit House of Correction. Her hair graying and her health deteriorating in captivity, Smith intimated that she had lied under oath, that the Cargins were innocent and that the guilty parties had escaped punishment. In 1880, Smith attempted to exonerate the Cargins with a deathbed confession, in which she admitted to lying under oath and insisted she knew nothing about the murder, which contradicted her earlier suggestion that she knew of guilty parties walking free. She died of stomach cancer on August 7, 1880.[7]

9. Julia Cargin, Saginaw, Life (1876, sentence commuted in 1885)

According to Mary Jane Smith's testimony during the murder trial, both she and her lover Nock Alexander wanted her cranky old husband out of the way, but neither had the fortitude to do it. So they enlisted the help of her sister Julia Cargin and Julia's husband, Freeman, in exchange for $500 (from the insurance on the barn they planned to burn with Smith's body inside). Either Mary Jane Smith lied to save her own skin during the 1876 trial, or she told a not-so-white lie four years later when she gave her penultimate confession. Perhaps moved by the belief that a dying woman would not lie, Governor Josiah Begole pardoned Julia Cargin in 1885. Begole left office before he had the chance to pardon Freeman Cargin, who remained in prison until Begole's successor Russell Alger pardoned him in 1886. Upon Freeman Cargin's release, the *Saginaw Courier-Herald* commented, "With due respect for the opinion of Gov. Alger…through executive clemency two of the principal actors in that dreadful tragedy have in a measure escaped the just penalty of their crime."[8]

10. Ellen Bemis, Ionia, Life (1881, pardoned in 1884)

Ellen Bemis said she had purchased strychnine at the request of her son-in-law, William Henderson, who wanted to kill muskrats. Somehow, the strychnine ended up in Henderson's stomach. His torso wish-boned as the poison overwhelmed his nervous system, and he died at the tender age of twenty-five. Bemis explained that Henderson must have died by suicide, but when an investigation uncovered bad blood between Bemis and her son-in-law, supposedly caused by alleged mistreatment of her daughter, Ellen Bemis found herself charged with murder. Convicted on tissue-thin evidence, Bemis's life sentence amounted to a mere four years when Governor Josiah Begole granted her a Christmas pardon on December 25, 1884.

11. Nettie Barnard, Montcalm, Acquitted

The cold-blooded murder of Reverend E. Curtiss's wife shocked the small town of Greenville. A well-liked preacher, the aged Curtiss had, according to local gossip, become particularly close with Nettie Barnard, the young wife of a local lumberman. Some of the reverend's flock had seen Curtiss strolling arm in arm with Mrs. Barnard, which caused tongues to wag and the rumor mill to churn out salacious stories about an affaire de coeur. The interest appears to have been one-sided, with Curtiss growing increasingly uncomfortable with the attention of his young parishioner. He moved to Lapeer, but she followed him, so he confronted the young wife and asked her to stop this stalker-like behavior.

In 1881, Curtiss's wife, Charlotte, died following a tragic house fire caused by an overturned kerosene lamp. Suspicion fell on Mrs. Barnard, whom local authorities believed doused Mrs. Curtiss's clothes with oil and started the fire so she could have the clergyman to herself. The strongest witness against Mrs. Barnard was the victim. As she lay dying, Charlotte Curtiss wrote out a dying declaration: "Mrs. Ezra P. Barnard came into my house after my husband went to church this evening and I told her to go away. She said that she would not, that she wanted to have a talk with me. She said I had wronged her and blew the light out; said she would have revenge and came right at me. She then threw gasoline all over me and into my mouth, and I soon saw that I was all on fire. I screamed and rolled over on the floor to try and put the fire out."[9]

The first trial, held in Lapeer, ended with a guilty verdict, but a successful appeal led to a second trial conducted in Charlotte, far away from the acerbic tongues of local yentas. Reverend Curtiss testified against Mrs. Barnard, but despite his strong belief in her guilt, the jury remained unmoved and unconvinced in the unlikely scenario of a young, attractive wife chasing a feeble, geriatric minister. The second trial ended in an acquittal.[10]

12. Koren Larson, Muskegon, Life (1884, pardoned in 1886)

Koren and Ole Larson faced murder charges for poisoning sixty-year-old John Guild with Rough on Rats, a rodenticide containing arsenic, to obtain the elderly man's money. Tried first, Koren received a life sentence on a case built from circumstantial evidence. The same evidence, however, did not convict her husband. Concerned about a possible miscarriage of justice, the Woman's Christian Temperance Union took up her case and pushed for a release. Koren Larson received a pardon in 1886.[11]

13. Elizabeth Vanderhoof, Berrien, Life (1884, sentence vacated in 1888)

In Galion, gossip swirled about an affair between Elizabeth Vanderhoof and her husband's hired man John Chapman. When William Vanderhoof died unexpectedly in December 1883, townsfolk suspected murder. An exhumation six weeks later appeared to prove it when Vanderhoof's stomach was found to contain arsenic. Convicted of poisoning her husband, Elizabeth's life sentence ended after four years when the Michigan Supreme Court overturned the guilty verdict and ordered a new trial. *The People v. Elizabeth Vanderhoof* died when prosecutors decided to spare the county the expense of a trial considered futile without any new evidence.

14. Etna Brass, Missaukee, Life (1886, pardoned in 1907)

Housewife Etna Brass was putty in the hands of handyman James Crafts. Not long after the two began an affair, Brass's husband, Miles, disappeared. Etna and James set up house in Cadillac, where James usurped Miles Brass's role as Etna's husband and father figure for her three children. When an investigation into Miles Brass's disappearance uncovered a partially buried body in the root cellar, Etna Brass and James Crafts pleaded guilty to murder and were both sentenced to life. After serving twenty-one years, Brass managed to convince the pardon board that Crafts, and not she, swung the flat-iron that brained Miles Brass. Governor Fred Warner commuted Brass's sentence to thirty-five years, which, considering time off for "good time" served, freed her in 1907. A frail woman, Etna Brass had lost twenty-five pounds during her twenty-one years, emerging from prison at an emaciated ninety pounds.[12]

15. Nellie Pope, Wayne, Life (1895, paroled in 1917)

Nellie Pope, the wife of prominent Detroit dentist Dr. Horace Pope, had acquired two very bad habits: a love of opium-laced medicines and a barber named William Brusseau, who shared his lover's affection for opium. When the dentist was drilling in the front parlor of their home and Billy was out acquiring drugs, Nellie took out life insurance policies on her husband amounting to a whopping $14,000. Then, she lured the dentist into their bedroom, where Billy crept up behind him and whacked him in the head several times with a hatchet. Supposedly asleep in the room where her father was killed, Berniece, obeying orders from her mother, helped wipe away the blood from the floor and walls. Both Nellie and Billy received life sentences for the plot. Billy died in captivity, but Nellie served twenty-two years before leaving prison on parole in 1917.[13]

Nellie Pope, circa 1890. *Author's collection.*

16. Mate Askins, Benzie, Life (1899, died in prison in 1903)

In 1899, twenty-nine-year-old widow Mate Askins confessed to poisoning her children—eight-year-old Glenn and twelve-year-old Margaret—to "get them out of the world." Described by one reporter as "not unfair of face and form, about medium height, and a pronounced blonde" with an "intellect as keen and ready as a briar bush," Askins struggled emotionally and financially when her husband died three years earlier. She purchased thirty grains of morphine, two ounces of carbolic acid and three ounces of cocaine from a Thompsonville pharmacy, then checked into a hotel. She mixed the morphine in glasses of sherry and served it to the children, who dutifully downed the poisoned concoction. Then she swallowed the rest of the poison and half of the cocaine but had second thoughts and cried for help. Glenn survived, but his older sister died from the overdose, which put Mate Askins on trial for murder. Glenn testified that his mother experimented with various poisons on stray dogs and cats. Sentenced to life, she died of tuberculosis in 1903, one day shy of exactly four years from her murder-suicide attempt.[14]

17. Sarah Quimby, Gratiot, Life (1901, paroled in 1918)

In 1901, Sara Quimby decided to leave the cold, cruel world and take her two children with her. She spiked a bottle of wine with morphine and served it to her kids before quaffing the remainder. She survived; her children didn't. When roused from the drug-induced stupor, Quimby blurted out a confession. "I'm a murderess," she said, "I expect to go to the penitentiary for life. The only request I have to make is that you allow me to see my children properly buried then I will go with you and take my sentence."[15] The jury agreed. She had served seventeen years of a life sentence when she received a parole in 1918. Her husband, eighty-six-year-old Elmer, convicted of complicity in the crime, died in prison of typhoid fever in 1901.[16]

18. Mary Murphy McKnight, Kalkaska, Life (1903, paroled in 1920)

Mary's biography reads like a twisted nursery rhyme: everywhere that Mary went, she left bodies in her wake. Her body count included two husbands; Dorothy Jenson, a little girl she baby-sat from time to time; her nineteen-year-old sister Sarah; and her brother John's entire branch of the Murphy family tree (his wife, Gertrude, and their daughter, Ruth). Arrested in 1903, Mary confessed to poisoning John, Gertrude and Ruth with strychnine, which she routinely took in small doses for medicinal use. Sentenced to life, Mary left prison on parole in 1920.

19. Caroline Collins, Shiawassee, Life (1903, sentence reversed in 1906)

According to local gossip, Carrie Collins was suspiciously close with her husband's farmhand George Leachman. Leachman died unexpectedly in 1903 after experiencing the symptoms of arsenical poisoning: a burning sensation in the stomach, an insatiable thirst and vomiting. When an analysis of his digestive organs revealed two-fifths of a grain of white arsenic, Collins ended up in the county jail awaiting her murder trial.[17]

The nonlethal amount of arsenic did not dissuade the jury, which convicted Collins of murder. Her life sentence ended three years later when the Supreme Court ordered a new trial. With no new evidence and very little chance of convicting Caroline Collins, the county prosecutor opted to drop the case.

20. Jennie Flood, Kent, Life (1903, paroled in 1916)

In 1903, the widow Flood was suspected of shooting handyman John London at point-blank range with a shotgun. Subsequent investigation revealed several life insurance applications, in Flood's handwriting, naming Flood as the beneficiary. The jury did not believe her story that she had scripted the applications for the barely literate farmhand and sent her to the Big House for life. She was gifted a Christmas parole by Governor Woodbridge Ferris in December 1916.

21. Carrie Joslyn, Ingham, Life (1905, paroled in 1918)

Carrie Joslyn had prepared an early Christmas gift for her husband William. On December 10, 1905, she served him arsenic-laced coffee in the first course of a two-week poison regimen to free herself so she could marry the hired hand Isaac Swan. When William Joslyn succumbed on December 24, 1905, suspicion immediately fell on the wife and her paramour, who apparently liked to kiss and tell. At Swan's trial, prosecutors introduced a witness who repeated Swan's graphic descriptions of romantic encounters he had had with the married woman. The testimony became so steamy, the judge ordered all women out of the courtroom. Both star-crossed lovers received life sentences. Swan was paroled in 1916; his former lover followed two years later in 1918. She died in Mason in 1932 at the age of fifty-nine.[18]

22. Mary Francis "Puss" Dewey, Washtenaw, Life (1912, paroled in 1961)

Dewey (dubbed "Puss" by her fellow inmates because she loved cats) had spent forty-nine years in prison when she finally received a parole and left prison at the age of eighty-five. Her life sentence stemmed from the murder of her adopted baby in 1912. Known at the time as Mrs. Bert Wildsmith, Dewey accused her husband of causing the injuries that led to the death of the ten-month-old boy, but two previous convictions for battering kids came back to haunt her. Sentenced to life, she was oldest female inmate in Michigan when the prison gates swung open for her in 1961. Her freedom lasted for only a few months; she died in April 1962.[19]

23. Mary Lucas, Ingham, Life (1913, pardoned in 1921)

When she purchased aconite from a Lansing druggist, boardinghouse maven Mary Lucas explained that she wanted the poison to dispatch a sick horse. About half an ounce of aconite ended up in hot cocoa she served to Paula Fingel, whom she believed had caught the eye of her sweetie John Berenze. During a subsequent confession, Mary Lucas said, "I did have a big horse in my way." Amid concerns about her sanity, she was convicted and received a life sentence, which ended in 1921 when outgoing Governor Albert Sleeper pardoned her. She was seventy-seven years old.[20]

24. Martha Steele, Muskegon, Life (1915, paroled in 1927)

When Prosecutor Harris E. Galpin recounted the grisly murder of eleven-year-old Evalina Steele, a woman in the courtroom fainted. Medical testimony established that Evalina's killer pulled out her tongue, poured hydrochloric acid down her throat and choked her to death. It took the jury an hour to determine that the fingermarks around Evalina's throat were made by the hands of her stepmother Martha Shrebe Steele, a seemingly motiveless crime that left court-goers wondering about her sanity. Steele went into the Detroit House of Correction at age thirty and emerged at age forty-one when Governor Alexander Groesbeck paroled her in 1927.[21]

25. Caroline Becker, Wayne, Life (1915, paroled in 1924)

Sixty-three-year-old Caroline Becker heard rumors that Frances Bumholt kept a mattress bank containing $50 in her house. As Mrs. Bumholt was on her knees praying, Becker crept up behind the unsuspecting woman and brained her with a chunk of heating coal. After rifling through the house, she managed to find just $15. When police arrested Becker, they found two blood-stained banknotes still in her shoe. "Aunty Caroline," as she was known by her fellow inmates, left prison in 1924 when Governor Alex Groesbeck issued her a parole.[22]

26. Carrie Hatton, Montcalm, Life (1918, paroled in 1923)

Forty-seven-year-old Carrie Hatton despised her husband William's binge drinking. She chided the tippler, which led to periodic rows. One particular argument in October 1918 turned deadly. According to Carrie, Hatton knocked her to the floor with a vicious right cross and threatened to silence her carping with an axe. She grabbed a .32-caliber handgun for protection and fired it to scare away the inebriated farmer, but she was too good of a shot. The bullet struck William Hatton in the right temple. Behind bars in the county jail, Carrie Hatton revised her statement and admitted that she had deliberately shot her husband but added a justification of sorts when she described his behavior as "beastial." The local press wouldn't print the particulars, instead offering a tantalizing clue: "She tells of some of the vile, low, unspeakable and unprintable things which Hatton, her husband, compelled her to do to satisfy his beastly cravings" She received a life sentence that ended five years later with her parole in 1923.[23]

27. Inez Johnson, Isabella, Life (1919, paroled in 1927)

The *Isabella County Enterprise* characterized the testimony against Inez Johnson as "nasty enough for almost any crowd" and showing "how degraded a human being can get in this land of decency." Johnson stood accused of luring young Beatrice Epler to her home in Alma and standing by while two male accomplices—Albert Eichorn and Joseph F. Brennan—dragged the sixteen-year-old into a bedroom and took turns raping her. Johnson was seen with Epler in the back seat of a car that would take her for a ride ending with her strangulation in a secluded field. Both Johnson and Eichorn received life sentences; Brennan beat the rap. Inez Johnson left prison in 1927 when she received a parole.[24]

28. Stanislava Lipczynska, Leelanau, Life (1919, pardoned in 1926)

After the skeleton of Sister Mary Janina—a murdered nun who disappeared eleven years earlier—surfaced in 1918, Sheriff John Kinnucan supposedly employed some theatrics in attempting to pry a confession from the lips of his prime suspect, parish housekeeper Stanislava Lipczynska. He asked the housekeeper if she would like to see Sister Janina and led her into a room lit by candles encircling a figure covered by a white sheet. The sheet was removed to reveal a skeleton, which Kinnucan had rigged with hinged jawbones. As he chanted "You killed me! You killed me!" the skeleton's jaws moved. Kinnucan's treatment of his suspect became a subject of debate at Lipczynska's murder trial in October 1919, which ended with a guilty verdict and a life sentence at hard labor in the Detroit House of Correction. Doubts about Lipczynska's guilt, which linger to this day, contributed to her pardon in 1926.[25]

29. Louise McKnight, Saginaw, Life (1921, paroled in 1934)

One of Manley McKnight's boarders recounted an incident that occurred a few hours before his landlord passed away unexpectedly. Manley's wife, Louise, served coffee with dinner. Upon sipping the brew, Manley complained about the bitter taste. He died the next day, which triggered murder charges against Louise. The case climaxed in June 1920 with a sensational trial before a standing-room-only crowd of the morbidly curious. A hung jury led to a second trial and a life sentence for the Saginaw housewife. Louise McKnight entered the House of Correction at about the same time that fellow poisoner Mary McKnight left on parole. Louise McKnight followed her namesake in 1934, when she too received a parole.[26]

30. Sarah Elizabeth Lewen, Wayne, Life (1921, died in prison in 1940)

Known in millinery circles as "Madame LeGrande," Lewen decided to even the score with Frank Ernest, an interested party in a real estate transaction who helped evict Lewen for nonpayment. She stalked his home and snatched his six-year-old son, Max Ernest, when he went out on his tricycle. Leading the boy to a secluded area, Lewen threw him to the ground, stomped on his forehead with a high-heel shoe (leaving three concentric circle marks on his forehead), stuffed his mouth with leaves and strangled him. Lewen was actually tried and convicted twice. The first verdict was nullified when she was judged insane. Following a stint at the state mental hospital in Ionia, she stood trial a second time. The second

Sarah Elizabeth Leuwen, or "Madam LeGrande," the milliner murderess. *Author's collection.*

guilty verdict sent her to prison for life. She died at the Detroit House of Correction in 1940 at the age of seventy-two. Just before she died, she told a confidant, "I'm not going to die. I just can't die until I am vindicated. I know there is a power of justice which will reveal the truth about me before I die."[27]

31. Meda Hodell, Newaygo, Life (1922, sentence commuted in 1949)

In 1922, Meda Hodell dosed her father-in-law's coffee with strychnine, reportedly to get rid of the feeble old man because he "required too much attention." Three months later, following an argument, she struck her husband, Romie, in the head with a rolling pin as he slept. But not hard enough. "Romie was still quivering," Meda reportedly confessed, "and mother, who was nearby, struck him again. He grew still." Alice Dudgeon then ordered her two sons to hang the body from barn rafters to simulate a suicide-by-hanging.[28]

Sentenced to life for the murder of her father-in-law David Hodell, Meda had served twenty-eight years when her sentence was commuted in 1949. She had entered prison at age twenty-one and left at age forty-seven.

Newaygo County sheriff Noble A. McKinley leads Meda Hodell into court in this press photograph from 1922. *Author's collection.*

32. Alice Dudgeon, Newaygo (hung jury in 1925)

Alice Dudgeon; her two sons Lee and Herman; and a farmhand named Robert Bennett were all suspected in playing some role in the bludgeoning of Romie Hodell and the attempted coverup. Perhaps taking a cue from Sheriff Kinnucan, state police officers obtained a confession from Dudgeon by staging a macabre tableau. At midnight, they brought her into the barn where a figure covered by a white sheet stood in a dark corner. The ghost of Romie Hodell—played by an "undercover" police officer—then accused Dudgeon of murder. The ploy worked; Alice Dudgeon signed a confession that she immediately repudiated, claiming the officers had obtained it under duress.

Meda Hodell's mother and fellow murder defendant Alice Dudgeon in a press photograph from 1922. *Author's collection.*

The confessions came back to haunt Alice Dudgeon and her two sons. Convicted for the murder of Romie Hodell, all three received life sentences, which the Michigan Supreme Court reversed. The legal odyssey would eventually take the three Dudgeons through four trials in three counties. Lee and Herman went free, leaving Alice Dudgeon to face the music alone. Following a hung jury in 1925, prosecutors decided to save the taxpayers the additional expense of any further trials and released her.[29]

33. Stella Blanche Mottl, Mason, Life (1920, pardoned in 1926)

Stella Blanche Mottl told the chemist she needed two ounces of white arsenic to poison a rat, but a jury found her guilty of putting them in Amel Mottl's salmon supper to free herself from a loveless marriage. Before, during and after the trial, Blanche maintained her innocence and claimed that Amel died by suicide. Governor Alexander Groesbeck pardoned the thirty-six-year-old in her sixth year of a life sentence.[30]

34. May Blenn Ford, Wayne, Acquitted (1922)

A cabaret dancer from Toledo, May Blenn met Plymouth farmer Ney Ford through a Lonely Hearts Club. Lured by the mistaken belief that Ford belonged to the superrich Henry Ford family, May agreed to marry Ney

Happily never after: Wedding announcement sent from the newlyweds Ney Ford and May Blenn Ford. *Author's collection.*

following a brief romance by mail. Upon discovering her husband's humble roots, the newly wedded bride commissioned a hitman named "Kansas City" Ed to widow her.

Little did she suspect as she met with "Kansas City" Ed and laid out plans for the hit that her contract killer was in fact Edward Kunnath of Detroit's Detective Bureau. Arrested for conspiracy to commit murder, May Blenn sidestepped a prison term when her lawyer managed to convince the twelve men on the jury that merely talking about plotting a husband's murder does not fulfill the legal definition of "conspiracy."

35. Maude Cushing Storick, Cass, Life (1923, pardoned in 1949)

Maude Cushing Storick had been married to her second husband, Emory Storick, for less than a month when she was arrested for poisoning her first husband, Claude Cushing. By the time of her release in 1949, she had spent more time in prison than any other Michigan woman. Governor G. Mennen Williams pardoned her in large part because, after the trial had concluded, evidence surfaced that Claude Cushing habitually took arsenic as a sort of cure-all and was even warned by a doctor that prolonged use of the drug could prove fatal. Storick was sixty-six years old when she left the Detroit House of Correction in 1949. Emory Storick, separated from his wife for nearly three decades, was waiting for her.[31]

36. Marjorie Kuhn, Hillsdale, Life (1923, discharged in 1925)

When examining the stomach and liver of Zelon Lake, chemist Charles B. Bliss discovered .52 grains of strychnine sulfate. Bliss fed a pinch of the poison to a mouse, which promptly dropped dead, and concluded that Lake had ingested a sufficient quantity to have killed him. Suspicion fell on Lake's common-law wife, forty-one-year-old Marjorie Kuhn, whose checkered past emerged during the investigation. Twice married, twice divorced and once imprisoned for bigamy, Kuhn became the likeliest suspect since Lake died after suffering from convulsions following a Christmas dinner. The complete lack of motive apparently did not deter the jury, which found Kuhn guilty as charged. Her life sentence ended two years later when the Michigan Supreme Court reversed her conviction on the grounds of insufficient evidence. The cloud of a second trial hovered until 1926, when the Hillsdale County prosecuting attorney decided not to pursue the case.[32]

37. Emma Kopple, Ingham, Life (1923, died in prison in 1945)

A few weeks before fourteen-year-old Harry Kopple's death, his foster mother Emma raised his life insurance amount by $500—from $1,200 to $1,700—and then fed him arsenic-laced candy. During the probe, investigators learned that Emma Kopple may have taken the boy from his mother in lieu of payment for a boarding bill. They also learned that she had been linked with as many as seven other deaths, most of them children, dating back to 1898, when a six-year-old orphan she fostered died after she kicked him out of the house in the dead of winter. The boy wobbled to a neighboring house, where the occupant tried to thaw his frozen feet and legs by inserting his limbs in an oven. He died a few days later, supposedly of diphtheria. Convicted of poisoning Harry Kopple, Emma Kopple's life sentence was just that: she died in the Detroit House of Correction in January 1945 at the age of eighty-one.[33]

38. Minera Abass, Wayne, Life (1924, discharged in 1936)

After serving a dozen years in prison for a crime she did not commit, forty-seven-year-old Minera Abass left the Detroit House of Correction in December 1936 with a monetary gift of twenty-five dollars and an apology from the state. One of the first things she did was go shopping with Warden Edward Denniston and his wife. She purchased a tweed sport coat fringed with a red fox collar.

In 1924, Minera Abass was convicted of engineering a conspiracy to murder her husband, affluent businessman Hussein. The assassin, Ahmed Mohammed, confessed to shooting Abass on the instructions of Minera, whom he said promised to marry him if he did the deed. He said that she had obtained the gun and had taught him how to shoot it. She watched as Mohammed shot her husband as he slept and then directed Mohammed to tie her up with suspenders to simulate a home invasion. In the twelfth year of his life sentence, Mohammed had a change of heart and admitted to lying in his confession, saying that Minera had had nothing to do with the murder.[34]

39. Euphemia Mondich, Wayne, Life
(1924, died in prison in 1961)

In prison, Euphemia Mondich was fond of gardening and feeding skunks enticed onto prison grounds by the odor of bread crumbs she left for the wildlife. She apparently had an affection for skunks, or so she led police to believe when they questioned her about the disappearance of her lover John Udorovich. When Euphemia Mondich began an affair with Udorovich, she had four ex-husbands, one of whom dropped out of sight after Udorovich brained him with a hammer and deposited the body in a dump. Then Udorovich disappeared. Arrested and grilled about her lover's vanishing, Euphemia said that she had shot her lover in self-defense and led police to the crawlspace under a cottage where she had stashed his body. The self-defense argument fell apart when investigators discovered three bullet wounds and two fractures at the top of the dead man's skull. After Euphemia Mondich received a life sentence, ex-husbands no. 2 and no. 4 said their farewells by way of gently shaking her hand. Outside of the courthouse, the two exes shook hands, congratulating each other on having survived her. She had spent thirty-seven years in prison when she died in April 1961 at the age of seventy-seven.[35]

40. Ethel Walker, Wayne, Life (1924, sentence commuted in 1936)

In June 1924, twenty-six-year-old Ethel Walker committed the ultimate Motown crime when she shot a friend, Kelly Meyers, over a dispute involving taste in music and a record collection. Sentenced to life, she left prison when her sentence was commuted in 1936.[36]

A composite of two pages from the 1900 U.S. Census listing the inmates in the female wing of the Detroit House of Correction. *National Archives and Records Administration.*

2
A DAY IN THE LIFE

JUNE 12-13, 1900

In July 1899, a Biograph photographer visited the Detroit House of Correction and managed to take a few pictures of the inmates as they walked single file to dinner. Two in the sequence of images, published in the July 16 edition of the *Detroit News*, provide a rare glimpse at daily life for the penitentiary's female population. In the words of a News writer, the lighting was ideal, "the whitewashed walls of the interior admirably reflecting the light and cutting out the deeper shadows."[37]

The result is a glimpse through a window into the past.

The inmates wore standard, prison-issued dresses made of a heavy-duty material and described by one reporter as "a striped blue and white seersucker goods, with large white apron and 'kerchief."[38] Consistent with socially acceptable women's apparel of the late nineteenth century, the hems of the dresses stretched to the ground. Following long-established prison rules, the women proceeded in single file and were not permitted to speak with one another. They may also have been required to fold their arms as they walked.

Only three characters are identified by name: Captain Joseph Nicholson, the prison superintendent; his wife; and infamous inmate Nellie Pope, who was convicted of conspiring to murder her husband in 1895. Pope refused to be photographed "unsupported," so Nicholson was a good sport and walked beside her. His wife, wearing a fashionable black dress, walks directly behind them. Known as a tall, "statuesque beauty," Pope stands a full head taller than the next tallest inmate and appears taller than Nicholson (without his hat).

An unnamed Biograph cameraman took two photographs of the House of Correction's female population as they marched to dinner in July 1899. That same month, the *Detroit News-Tribune* published the photographs as part of a collage. In the first photograph, lifer Nellie Pope walks side by side with Captain Joe Nicholson—the prison superintendent—who leads a procession of unidentified prisoners while a matron wearing a black dress brings up the rear. Nicholson's wife, also wearing a black dress, is walking behind him. *Library of Congress.*

Unfortunately, the identities of Pope's fellow inmates were casualties of publication restrictions; their names simply could not fit into a succinct photo caption.

"With so many figures in so small a space as a page of The News-Tribune supplement it is almost impossible to get likenesses," lamented the writer in charge of captioning the photo collage, "but doubtless not a few prisoners will be recognized by their shape, or swing, or some other familiar characteristic."[39]

Most of the unnamed women were serving time for wobbling through the streets, passing out on curbsides or fighting with fellow inebriates.

In a profile of "Captain Joe" and the prison published by the *Free Press* in 1890, Nicholson characterizes a majority of the female inmates as small-time serial offenders in and out of the House for drunk and disorderly conduct. These habitual prisoners came and went with some frequency. Nicholson pointed out one particular inmate to a curious reporter, who described her as an "old woman with a wrinkled, parchment face and white hair." The unnamed inmate was serving her 102nd stint for "the love of whiskey."[40]

Over a century has further blurred the identities of the nameless personages in the Biograph pictures, but a few clues can be found in the two pages documenting the residents in the 1900 federal census.[41]

Recorded on June 12–13, 1900, the census list was compiled less than a year after the Biograph photo, and except for a few short-timers whose sentences ended in the eleven-month interval and thus left the system, many of the women in the picture must also appear in the census record, which contains entries of fifty-nine female prisoners. While it is nearly impossible to match the names on the census list with the women in the photographs without additional photographic material for comparison, it is possible to place a few people inside the frame.

In June 1900, the prison housed four women who were lifers: Pope (line 21), Etna Brass (line 3), Mate Askins (line 13) and Fanny Echols (line 16). Brass, Askins and Echols almost certainly form part of the dinner procession.

Another face in the crowd belongs to Rose O'Donnell (line 1), a twenty-five-year-old described as "a professional shoplifter from Chicago." Her sticky fingers cost her two years and nine months behind bars when she was convicted in October 1898 in St. Joseph.[42] Somewhere inside the frame stands forty-nine-year-old Gertrude Smith (line 4), sentenced to two years for running a bordello in Detroit.

Lizzie Lawson (line 6) and Minerva Maxwell (line 8) were both doing time for drunk and disorderly. While Lawson is probably present in the photograph, Maxwell is certainly not; during the incident that led to her arrest and conviction, she became so inebriated that she passed out and hit her head on a curb. She spent part of her time in a local hospital and first entered the prison on July 30. She missed the photo op by about two weeks.[43]

Other inmates in July 1899 and likely present in one of the Biograph photos:

Mason resident Clara Thayer (line 9) was convicted of forgery in March 1899 and sentenced to five years.[44]

Dora Roberts (line 11) took part in relieving a bartender of $200, which led to her incarceration in 1898.[45]

In 1896, Alice Lane (line 15) began serving a sentence of ten years for manslaughter that stemmed from her role in the untimely demise of Emily Hall, who died after Dr. Dennis J. Seaman, assisted by Lane, performed an abortion.

By the time of the Biograph photo, Fanny Echols (line 16) had spent fifteen years behind bars, making her the inmate with the highest seniority. In 1884, she murdered her husband in a fit of rage. The crime, committed in Indian Territory, led to a sentence of death by hanging, but she escaped her date with the hangman when President Arthur commuted her sentence to life, so she joined other federal prisoners in the House. In 1899, a *Free Press* reporter described her as "a buxom, good-natured looking colored woman."[46]

Myrtle Brown (line 17) was convicted of pickpocketing in 1898.

Alice Lawrence (line 18) conspired to murder her husband in 1896. The fact that she did not deliver the blow killing her husband, Enos, probably saved her from a life sentence. Convicted of second-degree murder instead, she received a twenty-year prison sentence.

In May 1899, Carrie Ingersoll (line 20) and her husband, Harry, were convicted of torching a Lansing-area building to collect on the insurance. The female arsonist was sentenced to three years in the Detroit House of Correction.

Bessie Dickson (line 32) and Grace Mitchell (line 22) both received two-year sentences for robbing a local farmer. While awaiting sentence in the county jail, Dickson managed to escape by creating a dummy and then slipping out when the matron opened the cell door to deliver bread rations to Dickson and her cellmates.

Maggie Ross's (line 23) two-year sentence began in May 1898 when she was convicted of stealing fifty dollars' worth of clothes from her employer.

May Seymour (line 28) and a male accomplice by the name of Patrick Kain robbed a farmer in mid-March, 1899.[47]

Overseeing this motley crew fell largely on the prison's female guards, or matrons, one of whom appears in the Biograph pictures.

The willowy, forbidding figure in the black dress near the back of the procession in the first photograph and walking alongside the inmates in the second photograph is almost certainly Mrs. Brainard, the head matron, described by a *Free Press* reporter as "a tall, gentle woman, who does not by any means depend upon her physical force for protection."[48]

The photographs capture a moment in time and provide a rare glimpse at the women who called the House a home in July 1899.

3
TAKEN FOR A RIDE
BENTON HARBOR, 1924

With her bob and Mary Janes, doe-eyed teenager Florence McKinney looked more like the girl next door than a stone-cold killer. Whether she was a conniving murderess who would do anything for her man or nothing more than an innocent dupe depended on a conversation that she had had with her lover and confessed murderer Emil Zupke just before they took Cora Raber for a ride.

In August 1924, twenty-four-year-old Emil Zupke found himself in the middle of a love triangle. In one corner stood Cora Raber, the twenty-six-year-old daughter of a Glendora farmer. In the other stood nineteen-year-old Florence McKinney, whom Zupke described as "so much prettier and snappier" than her rival. Zupke was "crazy about" McKinney, he later said, and they planned to marry, but Raber was pressing him to put a ring on her finger instead.

Zupke, the son of a Berrien County farmer, was considered a good-looking but not tremendously bright fellow. Much to the chagrin of his father, he also had a lazy streak. Instead of rising with the cockcrow, he preferred to go drinking with his friends and sleep late. When he got a local girl pregnant, his father paid his way out of a "bastardy" charge. History would repeat itself with Cora Raber. The plain-Jane farm girl caught his eye; one thing led to another; and during the summer of 1924, she discovered that she was carrying Emil Zupke's child. She contemplated charging the deadbeat Zupke with bastardy but decided to give him a chance to do the right thing and marry her.

Cover girl: This photograph of nineteen-year-old Florence McKinney, one corner in a love triangle that turned deadly on a lonely country road, was published on the front page of the December 4, 1924 edition of the *Benton Harbor News-Palladium*. *Author's collection.*

The drama climaxed on a lonely country road on August 6, 1924.

Earlier that evening, Cora responded to a message from Zupke asking her to meet him at Knaack's drugstore.[49] He promised to marry her if she met him, but Zupke later explained that he used the marriage gambit as a lure. Instead of proposing matrimony, he said, he wanted "to talk things over with her" as he drove her back home.[50]

Titillated and relieved, the farmer's daughter dressed in her best white dress and new pair of canvas shoes. She pinned a gold wishbone pendant to her lapel to complete the ensemble. It was her favorite piece of jewelry.

Unsuspecting, Cora Raber climbed into Zupke's car. They motored down Lake Shore. When he came to the intersection of Lake Shore and Cleveland, Zupke turned toward Royalton, where Florence McKinney lived on her parents' farm. He would later describe it as a spur-of-the-moment decision. "But when I got on the Lake Shore," he explained, "I was thinking all the time of Florence and thought it would be lonesome driving back alone from Galien."

So he decided to pick up McKinney.

While en route, Zupke drove over something sharp that punctured one of the car's tires, so when he arrived at the McKinney household, he worked on patching the tires while Cora waited in the vehicle.

Realizing the awkwardness of the situation, Florence demanded that Zupke drive Raber back to Galien.

It was at this moment, Zupke confessed, that he first thought of doing away with Cora Raber.

"I had not thought of killing Cora until I had her at the McKinney home on the fatal night," he said without a scintilla of emotion in his tone. "While there mending the tires of my car I got to comparing the two girls. Florence was so much prettier and snappier that I thought I had to kill Cora to get her out of the way so I could marry Florence. I thought I had to have Florence and Cora wanted me to marry her. She was claiming I would be father of her baby when it would have been born."[51]

"I said, 'shoot, I'm not going to take her home.' And Florence asked me what I was going to do with her. I said, 'I don't know, kill her, maybe.'"

"And Florence said, 'Don't.' 'Well, you drive the car and I will take care of the rest,' I said to Florence. Then she looked at me and said, 'Ace, I'll do anything for you.'"

Florence slid behind the steering wheel while Zupke squeezed into the front seat next to Raber (his Star roadster had a single seat). McKinney later claimed that she had no idea what Zupke had in mind for the pregnant woman—a contention that Emil Zupke found incredulous.

"If Florence didn't know I intended to kill Cora when we all drove away from her house I don't know what she could have thought."

Zupke, however, had no doubts. By his own admission, he planned to kill Cora "on the Tamarack road," but his fraying nerves got the best of him. They motored on awhile. At the hamlet of Arden—northwest of Berrien Springs—they turned down a dirt road. At a desolate spot between two mint farms, Zupke jammed his forearm against Cora's neck.

"I was sitting with my right hand around Cora and my back partly turned to Florence," he told investigators.

> We were wedged in pretty tight. I had my legs partly over Cora's. Cora was rather slumped down in the car, as we had to sit that way. I took Cora by the shoulders and pulled her head back. She asked me what I was going to do. I did not answer, just began pulling my right arm out from under her back. She seemed to think she was all right. I put my right arm over her chest. Her hands were in her lap. I braced my left foot against the foot board and pressed my right elbow stiffly against her throat.

He leaned in, using his body weight for leverage. The force caused her head to go through the rear curtain of the car. Cora clawed at the muscled arm bar across her throat in a desperate attempt to free herself from Zupke's chokehold. Her body twitched, stiffened and then went limp like a deflated bag.

Zupke later tried to downplay the violent incident. "Cora did not seem to struggle," Zupke said. "If she did I did not notice. I was so excited and shaky, and the road was rough, too. I continued to press her throat with my elbow while we drove more than a mile." He held the fatal arm bar for twelve minutes.[52]

"Once when Cora gasped a little Florence asked me what I was doing and I said I was not hurting her....We were near the Hollywood road when I let go and she laid still with her eyes closed and mouth open."[53]

According to Zupke, both he and Florence believed that Cora Raber was dead, although Zupke also said that he made a futile attempt to revive Cora, and Florence said that she suspected Cora was alive and asked "Ace" to take her to a hospital. Unsuccessful in his attempts to resuscitate Cora and apparently under the assumption that she had breathed her last, Zupke dumped the corpse in an isolated area next to some railroad tracks.

"When I left her I laid her out pretty, as Florence wanted me to do," Zupke later said. He positioned the body so that Cora was lying on her left side with "the clothing neatly arranged." The body was discovered lying face down with her head resting on her right arm and her dress hiked up to her waist. The movement of the body was enough to convince Zupke that Cora Raber was alive when they left her in the tangle of underbrush.

The corpse lay undiscovered for four days. On August 10, a local farmer found the decomposing remains next to the Michigan Central railroad tracks. Cora Raber, apparently under the impression she was going to her wedding, was wearing a dress and a pair of new white canvas shoes.

Determining cause of death was tricky. In the days Raber's body lay undetected, animals had gnawed at it and obliterated much of her neck structures. Her eyes were missing, and there was damage to her face beyond that explained by four days of decomposing in the heat, which led to speculation that she had been beaten during a life-and-death struggle or that her killer had mutilated her, possibly with acid, to prevent identification.[54] Berrien County sheriff George C. Bridgman later said that her neck had been broken, and it appeared likely that she suffered from convulsions before she died.[55]

The trail inevitably led to Raber's sweetheart. Within hours of the body's discovery, Zupke was arrested and taken to the county jail, where he made a detailed confession to Sheriff Bridgman. At first, he said he had murdered Cora Raber soon after he picked her up at the drugstore. In this version of events, only after dumping her body did he swing by the McKinney residence.

Later that night, Florence McKinney turned herself in at the county jail and gave a statement containing a much-different version of events. She was in the car when Zupke killed Raber, but she insisted she had nothing to do with the murder and had no idea that it was going to happen. She merely drove the car.

At one point, she even swore she didn't know it was happening at the time. "While driving down this last dirt road," she told Sheriff Bridgman, "I heard Cora gasp once or twice. I said, 'Ace, what are you doing?' Emil said, 'Never mind, honey, I'm not going to hurt her.' But I saw his hand was at her throat and tried to pull it down. Emil said she was all right. Then he rode with his back to me. As we drove along I heard her gasp and asked him what he had done to Cora, and he said she was all right."[56]

Yet Zupke's Star roadster had one seat, so the three characters of the love triangle squeezed together in the front seat, most likely with Raber sitting on Zupke's lap. It seemed incredible that Florence did not recognize the violent act occurring right next to her, especially since

Zupke pushed on Cora's neck with such force that they broke through the back of the seat.[57]

Besides, Zupke did not appear to have the intelligence to plan such a crime. "They believe that he is incapable of planning so horrible an outrage," wrote a *Detroit Free Press* reporter in an exposé of the case published in the August 24, 1924 edition.[58] This speculation led some to suspect that despite her protests, Florence McKinney plotted Cora Raber's murder.[59]

And of the two suspects, Florence appeared more stolid and in control.

She was also a subject of tremendous curiosity to reporters. Interviewing her at the county jail, a *Herald-Press* reporter described the nineteen-year-old thus: "A slip of a girl, her large blue eyes peer forth from beneath her Dutch-bobbed hair in genuine frankness. She flits back and forth in her cell in girlish fashion, occasionally kidding the reporters in slang terms known to the present crop of flappers."[60]

Confronted with Florence McKinney's statement, Emil Zupke gave a second, amended confession to County Prosecutor Charles W. Gore and a court stenographer.[61] He had tried to shield McKinney, but now he swore to tell the truth. He drove Raber to the McKinney residence, where he told Florence that he planned to kill Cora and asked her to drive the car. Following the confession, he took a contingent of authorities and newspapermen on a tour of the "death route," which included a reenactment of the murder with one of the reporters standing in as the victim.

Zupke said that he intended to shield Florence and take the rap for the murder. "Florence and I agreed that I would take all the blame if worse came to worst," he said after the macabre tour. "She said she would wait for me until I served my time and I was free again, and then she would marry me. She said that night, "For heaven's sake, Ace, if you do get caught keep me out of it. But you got me to tell the whole story, and now I'm glad it is cleared up. I feel better to have it off my mind."[62]

Florence, however, expressed anything but love when she gave an interview from her cell. Characterizing herself as a victim, she exclaimed, "I feel that I have been more wronged than Cora Raber was." She described Zupke as a coward whom she believed incapable of murder. "It didn't occur to me he would kill her, because he was so chicken-hearted I wouldn't have thought he had the nerve. He always was yellow."[63]

"He did me a terrible wrong to get me into this mess," Florence said, "but he was always nice to me when we were going together. My slightest wish was law to him. He would get me anything I hinted I wanted."

"I wish he had killed me instead of Cora," Florence concluded, "then I would come back and haunt him." The unnamed reporter described a "wry smile" on Florence's lips as she contemplated this spectral revenge.[64]

Florence believed that they were driving Cora Raber to St. Joseph. "At Arden," she recalled, "he again told me to turn right. I did. But if I had known he was going to kill Cora on that road I certainly should not have let him take her there. I should have stopped and got some help somewhere. I would not have let him kill her."[65]

Florence's denials went unheard. Zupke's confession put her in front of a first-degree murder charge and possible life sentence.

The case became a sensation in Berrien County and dominated headlines throughout August 1924. At one point, a reporter compared Florence McKinney's emotional coolness to that of Leopold and Loeb, whose trial was taking place in Chicago while the doomed lovers awaited their time in court from cells in the Berrien County Jail.[66]

Florence McKinney became a press darling. Reporters reveled in the fact that the one-time Sunday school teacher with the "winsome smile" had become entangled in a love triangle that ended with her driving the roadster that took her rival for a ride. She attempted to keep a cheerful façade, but rings around bloodshot eyes told of sleepless nights spent sobbing.

The turning point of the entire case occurred on Wednesday, August 13, when a curious scene occurred in the office of Sheriff Bridgman. Just before the two defendants were brought in front of Justice Ray W. Davis for the arraignment, they were allowed to face each other for the first time since their arrests. Zupke and McKinney discussed what words they exchanged before motoring away in Zupke's automobile. In essence, they were allowed the opportunity to square their differing accounts of that pivotal moment on which McKinney's guilt in the murder balanced.

Whereas Zupke insisted in his formal confession that he told McKinney he planned on killing Cora Raber, he now relented and agreed that the language was vague and allowed for more than one interpretation. "I'll fix her so she will not bother me any more," he now insisted he said. This was a direct contradiction to his previous confession and a later statement he made to a reporter during the reenactment, when he said that he answered Florence's question with "I don't know, kill her, maybe."

They also agreed that when Florence asked Zupke, "What are you going to do, something so she will lose the baby?" Zupke responded, "I will not hurt her."[67]

Florence pleaded not guilty to the first-degree murder charge. Her case hinged on convincing a jury that she did not know Zupke intended on killing Cora Raber, which meant that the trial's focus would become a "he said, she said" account of that conversation they had in her parents' driveway as Zupke tended to the damaged tires.

As damning as Zupke's initial confession appeared for Florence, his statements were tempered with minor inconsistencies. In the words of one reporter, Florence McKinney was more lucid. "Emil does not think as fast as Florence," a reporter remarked with his tongue planted in his cheek. "His memory does not appear to be as vivid as hers."[68]

Convinced that Florence was more than an innocent dupe, the prosecution called Emil Zupke to testify at her preliminary hearing. Once again, the key testimony involved the words the accused murderers exchanged while Cora Raber waited in the car.

Zupke kept to the script. He said that he first planned on murdering Raber during that conversation, an admission that at first appeared detrimental to Florence's defense. But when Florence asked him what he planned to do, he testified to responding in vague language that was open to interpretation. "I told her," Zupke testified, "that I would take care of her so she won't bother me any more." He also said, "I told her I was not going to hurt her."[69] Zupke's turn on the stand helped rather than hindered Florence McKinney's defense.

The first-degree murder charge lingered over Florence McKinney until December, when the case came to an anticlimactic conclusion. What was expected to be "one of the most sensational murder trials in the history of this state" instead fizzled when McKinney pleaded guilty to the second count on the indictment, acting as an accessory after the fact.

The plea cheated locals of the high court drama they expected. In the words of a *News-Palladium* correspondent, "By so pleading, she not only avoided a sensational trial and possible conviction (which might have carried a life sentence) but she made certain that the part she played in the most sensational of all Berrien murders will call for a comparatively light sentence."[70]

"Comparatively light" was an understatement. She received a sentence of between one and seven years. A model prisoner in the Detroit House of Correction, she was paroled in 1926 after serving just one year.

One reporter's characterization of the pretty teenager as she stood and received her sentence was less than complimentary.

"Florence McKinney has been called brazen. She isn't. She simply displays no emotion. She did not take her arrest seriously. She joked about the 'inconvenience' of being locked up in the county jail until bail was obtained. Today she was the same, smiling coquettishly. No tragedy was written in her big eyes."[71] The reporter's ire may have resulted from Florence's refusal to say anything to the press other than "I haven't anything to say about it."

A few days after Florence McKinney's day in court, Emil Zupke, convicted of first-degree murder, went in front of Judge Charles E. White to receive the expected sentence of life.

One final twist in the case occurred in 1935, when, following a recommendation from the parole board, which in turn followed the recommendation of sentencing judge Charles E. White, Governor Frank Fitzgerald commuted Zupke's sentence to fifteen years.

In his recommendation to the parole board, Judge White cited his doubts about Zupke's confession and subsequent guilt. "The original story told by Zupke," White wrote in a letter to the parole board, "was so extremely improbable and unlikely that it cast a grave doubt in my mind as to whether or not Zupke was telling the truth or was endeavoring to protect some one."[72] White, however, did not name a possible "some one."

That someone, according to the rumor mill, was a doctor who performed an abortion on Cora Raber. When she died on the operating table, Zupke took the rap in exchange for a payment. In this scenario, Raber was dead before Zupke met with Florence McKinney. Sheriff Bridgman characterized the rumor as rot and cited damage to the back of the car seat as proof that Zupke murdered Raber.

Emil Zupke left prison on parole in 1935, but he couldn't keep his nose clean. In 1938, he faced charges of sending letters to the late sheriff George Bridgman's sister (Bridgman died in July 1936) demanding hush payment of $15,000 to not go public with an unpublished story relating to the Raber murder that presumably cast the late sheriff in a negative light. Found guilty in federal court, Zupke was sentenced to five years in Fort Leavenworth.

After serving his term in Kansas, he was returned to the state penitentiary at Jackson, where he served another twelve years for violating parole. In 1959, he faced negligent homicide charges following a fatal car accident that claimed the life of a twenty-two-year-old mother but avoided prison and served three years of probation instead. He died on January 4, 1973, at the age of seventy-two.[73]

Florence McKinney died on August 13, 1968, at the age of sixty-three. If she knew something about Zupke's plan to murder Cora Raber, she took that secret to the grave.

4

FOR SERVICES RENDERED

NILES, 1928

When the courtroom doors opened to begin the afternoon session on Wednesday, June 6, 1928, a rush of eager spectators flooded into the gallery. The modest room quickly filled. "Many stood on window sills and in the aisles," wrote one incredulous news correspondent. "Ante-rooms off the courtroom were also jammed."[74] The standing-room-only crowd had come to watch what they hoped would be the best drama in town—a lurid story of a pretty brunette secretary, her much older lover and an affair that ended with a single bullet from a .38. The "thrill seekers" hoped that when Marguerite "Deetie" Bumbaugh took the stand that afternoon, she would leave no details of her illicit affair with Walter Cook to the imagination.

On the morning of March 30, 1928, Deetie marched into Cook's factory with two of her brothers, Harry and Judd, and a loaded revolver.

Cook was dictating a letter to his secretary, a stunner named Helen Logan who won the "Miss Niles" title at the 1927 Blossom Festival beauty pageant. "Deetie," Myers later testified, "sort of smiled" as she entered the office with gun in hand and demanded payment for the money she believed Cook owed her. Cook said he would go straight to the bank and darted out of the office.

Deetie called him a "filthy reptile." She ran after him and shrieked, "Come on back here or I'll kill you, damn you!"

"Oh, no, you wouldn't do that," Cook retorted.

"Yes I will!" Deetie declared, pointing the .38 at the quivering man.

Marguerite Bumbaugh. *Library of Congress.*

She fired four times. The first shot ended up embedded in the floor. Just as she squeezed the trigger a second time, one of Cook's employees—E.R. Bath—slapped at her hand, and the bullet hit a wall. Bath would later testify that after the second shot, Judd Bumbaugh jabbed the barrel of his .38 into his ribs and warned him not to interfere. The third shot missed Cook and hit Thomas Harrison, the factory foreman, in the leg. The fourth hit Cook in the stomach, tearing through his liver. According to Helen Logan, Deetie demanded she bring a checkbook and commanded her to write out a check as her boss lay dying.

Deetie was arrested on the spot while Cook was transported to a local hospital. Twisting in pain, he managed to utter a final statement, in which he declared that he did not owe Deetie anything; she had invested in his lumber mill business, but after he declared bankruptcy, he did not have the means to pay her. He died later that day at the age of forty-four.[75]

In the hours after Cook's murder, the Niles Police Department received several enigmatic telephone calls indicating that "Cook had it coming."

Cook's slaying landed Deetie and her two brothers in court facing premeditated murder charges and possible life sentences.

There was never any doubt that Deetie fired the fatal shot. In fact, she signed a statement admitting to shooting Cook but added a flimsy self-defense caveat by stating that she pulled the trigger only after he had struck her in the head with a wicker basket. When asked why she shot instead of sued, Deetie demurred and said only that she worked for Cook as his private secretary.

Her poker face cracked when she was asked whether or not her boss conducted "himself as a gentleman." A reporter who witnessed this exchange spotted a peculiar expression. "A faint shadow of a smile parted her lips."

"If you don't mind, I'd rather not answer that question," Deetie replied. She was evidently hiding something.[76]

But Deetie knew that she would eventually need to answer that question. To avoid a life sentence, she would rely on an insanity defense, which meant she would have to convince a jury that Cook drove her beyond the brink of sanity. Her defense strategy was succinctly encapsulated in a statement she gave to her lawyers: "I didn't go there to kill him, but when I saw him all those terrible things he had done came back before my eyes and I went mad. I didn't know I had killed him until the police came."

To make her case, Deetie would need to pull back the sheets on a decade-long affair, to make public all "those terrible things he had done," which included no fewer than four back-alley abortions conducted by none other than Cook himself. The more graphic the testimony, the more convincing it would be to an all-male jury who may associate the defendant with their daughters or nieces.[77] The perpetrator would need to appear the victim, and the victim would need to appear the perpetrator. She would depict Walter H. Cook as a sex-crazed, womanizing deviant, which may have been more or less the truth. How much more and how much less would be a question for the jurors. Without Walter Cook to defend himself, the trial would not be a "he said, she said" but just a "she said."

And she said plenty.

According to defense attorney Edwin Donahue, Deetie began speaking through two poems she had written, which he believed proved her teetering mental state. The first, penned about six weeks before Cook's slaying, was aptly titled "The Maniac."

There is no peace,
   There is no Rest,
For Hope has died within my breast,
I fume and seethe in vain turmoil,
There is no Gain, There is no Spoil.
   For Hope has died!
   But left this shell,
A volcano of Moulten [sic] Hell!
   I sit as though
   In calm repose,
My tearless eyes refuse to close
While back and forth the World goes
   And laughs! Or Cries!
   Or never shows
The aching hearts—benumbed by blows
   Until Hope Dies!
   I know no Pain
   Since Hope is slain
And day or night is all the same;
My soul-less face looks forth, inane.
   Why! even you
   Could come or go,
I could not care, I would not know
   Love only strikes
   One Fatal Blow.[78]

Deetie wrote a second poem while she whiled away the time on the second story of the Berrien County Jail. Titled "Resurrection," the poem contained these lines:

Pity me? Why pity me
   Do you not know my Soul is Free!
   It is so hard for you to see

That human hands no longer hold
My Spirit
In their blinding fold?

Prosecutor George H. Bookwalter planned to smash Deetie's insanity defense by proving that she had a mercenary motive for the killing: Cook owed her money, plain and simple, and when he refused to take her to the bank and settle the alleged debt of $3,379.72, she shot him. Characterizing Deetie as more of a highwayman than a lover scorned, Bookwalter declared in his opening statement, "To her it was a case of money or your life and she took both." The only reason Deetie pleaded not guilty by reason of "temporary maniacal insanity," he argued, was so she could take the stand and air the dirty laundry of her affair with her boss.

In fact, Bookwalter pointed out, Cook did not owe her one red cent. In his dying declaration, Cook said that Deetie lost the money that she had invested in his failed lumber mill.

And then there was the fact that Deetie came to the factory carrying a loaded revolver. That she purchased the gun in California six days before the murder suggested premeditation.

Cook's secretary Helen Logan—who looked enough like Deetie to pass as her sister—took the stand as the prosecution's first witness. Logan was in the office taking dictation and witnessed the confrontation and the subsequent shooting. Her description of the defendant as pleasant and smiling when she entered the office did not help Deetie's case. Even more damaging to Deetie's insanity defense was Logan's testimony about her orders to fetch a checkbook, write out a check and sign both her and Cook's name to it—an amazingly lucid action for someone suffering from "temporary maniacal insanity."

Judd Bumbaugh also carried a gun—a .32-caliber pistol—the barrel of which he supposedly jabbed into the ribs of a worker who attempted to interfere, and commanded, "Let that girl alone."

Before summoning his star witness to the stand, Bookwalter called six eyewitnesses—teenaged basket weavers at Cook's Ultra-Nu Basket Factory—who testified to seeing Deetie chase Cook, fire at him four times and then force him to ink a check as he lay writhing in pain from the gut shot.

Bookwalter then called Elmer Latz, the lynchpin of his case for premeditated murder. Latz testified to selling the gun to Deetie in Los Angeles on March 24. Latz explained how Deetie told him she wanted the gun for self-defense after she had been robbed. He then told of accompanying her to a rifle range where she practiced with the pistol.

Four Ultra-Nu employees testified to hearing Harry Bumbaugh utter a statement that, the prosecutor hoped, would convince jurors that the trio planned to murder Cook before they came to Ultra-Nu on March 30. He allegedly said to Niles police chief George Francis, "That's all right, go ahead and arrest us because we expected that when we came here."

Another employee said he heard Harry Bumbaugh remark, "Well Cook, there's a settlement for everything."[79]

But the prosecutor's case suffered a setback: Chief Francis denied hearing Harry Bumbaugh make such a statement. When Francis replied "no," to Donahue's question during cross-examination, a reporter thought he saw a "faint smile—one of relief and hope—pass over Deetie's face."[80]

Bookwalter's case was short and to the point. He rested after just one day of testimony.

Deetie's defense attorney Edwin J. Donahue set the stage for his star witness by outlining his client's life story. To the shock and delight of the "thrill seekers" in the gallery, Donahue did not shy away from graphic depictions, which the press described as "replete with acts so revolting as to make most of it unprintable"[81]

The attorney also outlined the basis for Deetie's insanity defense. "When Marguerite Bumbaugh walked into Cook's office that day and shot him," Donahue explained in his opening statement, "she was the victim of an insane delusion that he was attempting to renew those terrible indecencies. She thought Cook was bearing down upon her mad with lust and she shot at his knee in self-defense."[82]

The apex of the trial took place when thirty-one-year-old Deetie Bumbaugh, doing her best Clara Bow impression, took the stand.[83] The defendant was dressed to the nines for her day in court: she wore a mink-collared coat over a navy blue dress, the ensemble topped by a white brocade hat with chocolate tangles of hair spilling from underneath the brim. Large, soulful eyes and dimpled cheeks gave her a little-girl look, which made her a sympathetic figure.

Her voice cracking and at times giving way to periods of heavy sobbing, Deetie struggled through the sordid tale of a love affair with her boss, a story that cast Cook as a manipulative Svengali and herself as his love slave.

The murder was the final act in a drama that began more than a decade earlier when eighteen-year-old Marguerite Bumbaugh went to work for Cook, who owned a sawmill in Warsaw, Indiana. According to Deetie,

Cook recruited her even though she had no experience, suggesting that the young, raven-haired beauty had caught the lumberman's eye during some previous encounter.

Six weeks after taking the job in the lumber mill, Deetie said, Cook asked her to report to work in the evening, which she dutifully did. She arrived to find the mill dark because the lights had failed. Cook offered to drive her home, so Deetie climbed into the back seat of his car. "He drove past my home and out into the country where he parked the car and got in the back seat with me," she testified. "He started caressing me, and I fought him off but I was not strong enough. He ripped my clothes from my body. I don't know—I know he was…well, I guess I was unconscious and then I came to and realized what a horrible thing had happened."[84]

Deetie threatened to tell her parents about the rape, but the silver-tongued Cook coaxed her into silence. Deetie described the conversation.

"Don't do that. I love you. I want to marry you," Cook said.

"I don't love you. You're too old," Deetie replied. Cook was thirty-one.

"Don't say that," Cook replied. "Ever since I've seen you at school I knew you were my girl. You are mine now."

"But you're married," Deetie reminded him. Cook then apparently said some disparaging words about his wife, Lena, words that she did not want to repeat even though Cook's widow retreated to the witness room when Deetie took the stand. Deetie pleaded with her lawyer. "Please, Mr. Donahue, I don't have to tell the things he said about his wife, do I?"

"Go ahead, tell just what happened," Donahue said.

"He said he and Mrs. Cook hadn't got along together for a long time. He said he didn't love her; that she had been threatening to get a divorce for the past two years, and now he'd let her get it, and marry me."

"And did that intimacy with him continue after that?" Donahue asked.

"Yes, practically every day. I didn't refuse him after that." She also gave in when Cook asked her not to cash her checks, so he could use the money instead. According to Deetie, Cook held her captive by continual promises to leave his wife and make her the next Mrs. Cook.

Sometimes Cook took her on weekend jaunts to Chicago, Grand Rapids and Indianapolis. Sometimes, he signed the hotel registers "W.H. Cook and wife." When Deetie discovered she was pregnant, Cook laughed, and she testified that he said he would "fix me up." He had once studied to be a doctor and knew what to do. According to Deetie, Cook "fixed her up" by performing an abortion with a wire in his office. A subsequent pregnancy a few years into the relationship led to a second wire-hanger abortion.

Deetie's health deteriorated following the second abortion. "I became so run down in health," she said, "I told him something had to be done." She took his advice and retreated to a friend's farm, but the rest and relaxation did her little good.

"I couldn't sleep nights," Deetie explained. "I was nervous, melancholy and blue. I couldn't concentrate on anything. I tried to read, to sew, but I couldn't keep my mind to it."

Noticing the changes, Cook accused Deetie of having a sexually transmitted disease and berated her for giving it to him, yet he would not allow her to see a physician. He was afraid that a doctor's visit would expose his extramarital relationships and possibly his work as a backroom abortionist. Deetie disobeyed and went to a doctor anyway. She underwent six treatments, but Cook refused to pick up the $150 tab.

According to Deetie, Cook railed at the doctor's bill and declared, "He's getting in a hell of a hurry for his money when I'm sending him a lot of business." The "lot of business" suggested that Cook's other lady friends had preceded Bumbaugh to the physician's table to receive treatment.[85] According to Deetie, the physician told her that Cook was receiving treatment for the same ailment. He eventually acquiesced and paid the physician in lumber.

A third pregnancy in 1923 led to a third abortion, once again performed by Cook.

Cook impregnated Deetie for a fourth time a year later. This time, she wanted to have the child. "I begged him to give me $500 that I might go away someplace where I wasn't known, and bear my child," she said. "He laughed in my face, saying he 'didn't want any children running around bearing his name.'"

At this point during her testimony, Deetie became overwhelmed with emotion. She paused to choke back her tears. After regaining her composure, she continued. "I pleaded with him to do something, to let me go to a doctor. I was afraid of another operation by him. He called me a coward. He said he wouldn't give me any money, but would perform another operation. In desperation I gave in."

The fourth wire-hanger abortion left Deetie with a life-threatening blood infection. She reposed at her brother Judd's house. Wiping tears from her cheeks, Deetie explained that she was terrified that her parents would find out. She didn't want to "break their hearts."[86]

Deetie survived the ordeal and decided on a fresh start about as far away from Walter Cook as she could go. In 1925, she left Ultra-Nu and Walter

Cook behind, moving to Los Angeles, California, but she did not forget the debt he owed her from unpaid wages and medical bills. She calculated the exact amount down to the penny: $3,379.72.

In December 1927, Deetie wrote one final letter to Cook in which she established deadlines for her deadbeat ex-lover to pay his debt. The letter, obtained and published by the *News-Palladium*, contained a few ominous lines. "Bear in mind that you are not dealing with the Marguerite Bumbaugh whom you betrayed, deceived, and robbed under the promise of marriage," she warned.

She characterized Cook as a rat. "Now," she continued, "on the chance that you have as much intelligence as the rat that you are (for even a rat knows when to seek safety) I am giving you until Jan. 1, 1928, to redeem this note. Also, I am giving you until Feb. 2, 1928, to pay me the other $1,027.62 cash that you owe me for salary for which you gave me post-dated checks."

Deetie ended her note with an ultimatum: "But remember this, if you do not pay this note and interest I am coming back to collect in person and I will make you pay me all of my money which you owe me which I loaned you from my earnings."[87]

Cook did not heed Deetie's warning, so she made good on her threat to "collect in person," which she attempted to do on March 30, 1928. She brought the gun, she said, because Cook threatened to kill her if she tried to collect.

Those who came to witness some theatrics did not leave disappointed. During Bookwalter's cross-examination, Deetie had an emotional breakdown in a scene that a journalist described as "the wildest scene ever enacted in the Berrien county court."

Observers feared just such a breakdown. Deetie had spent two months in a jail cell, and the specter of a life sentence had affected her appearance. Strands of steel gray appeared in her chestnut-colored hair; the laugh lines around her mouth and at the edges of her eyes had deepened and become visible; and dark circles made her eyes appear sunken and gave her a skeletal appearance.

After six hours on the stand spanning two court sessions over two days, she teetered on the brink of a breakdown, which finally came after Bookwalter read excerpts of Deetie's love letters to Cook and attempted to pry an admission from her that she attempted to persuade Cook to leave his wife. The question that appeared to send Deetie over the edge occurred when Bookwalter asked, "As a matter of fact Miss Bumbaugh, wasn't it just as much your fault as Cook's that you maintained and continued these relations?"

"I loved him—I loved him. I loved him until that trip to Chicago when he told me there were three other girls in his life. But I loved him and I belonged to him. I had given him my all," Deetie shrieked.

The admission unhinged her. "Suddenly she sprang from the witness chair," wrote a shocked journalist, "and then stretched out her tightly clenched fists toward the stunned spectators."

"Mother! Mother!" Deetie wailed. "Don't let them take the boys [her brothers]! They can take me but spare the boys."

Her brother Harry wrapped his arms around her, "but," wrote the *Herald-Press* correspondent who witnessed the pathetic scene, "with the strength of a mad person she broke from his arms and staggering to the jury box she shook her fists before the motionless body of her peers, screaming wildly."

"Do what you want with me—take me away—kill me!" she howled and repeatedly thumped her chest with her clenched fist for effect. "But spare my brothers! They have done nothing wrong."

Her brothers and parents, who watched the trial from the first row behind the defendants, encircled her. Her mother whispered something into her ear that had a calming effect.

While a bailiff escorted Deetie from the courtroom to the judge's chamber, where a doctor tended to her, the contingent of deputies attempted to restore order to the court.

When Deetie returned to the courtroom twenty minutes later, she was white as a sheet and visibly trembling. She sat next to her brother Harry, and the trial continued.

Donahue called Dr. Fred N. Bonine to the stand.

Bonine, who had visited with Deetie in jail, concluded that she suffered from a condition he labeled "paranoia," which he defined as "an affection of the brain, causing the person to be the opposite of sane—or insane."

According to Bonine, Deetie suffered from delusions that resulted from years of abuse at the hands of Walter Cook. When she went to the Ultra-Nu factory to confront her former lover, all the negative memories flooded her and she imagined him attacking her. The fact that he didn't—established by numerous eyewitnesses—only further proved her delusions.

Despite her moving narrative, Deetie may have felt that she was swimming against the current. On Friday, June 8, she made a deal with the prosecution. After a two-hour conference between Donahue and Bookwalter, she agreed to drop her insanity defense and instead plead guilty to manslaughter. In return, Prosecutor George H. Bookwalter agreed to drop all charges against her brothers. Donahue later told reporters that Deetie's decision to accept a prison term was in part motivated by the desire to see her older brothers freed.

Although it may have seemed anticlimactic to veteran court-goers, everyone appeared pleased with the outcome. Deetie beamed. Harry and Judd wept, and the spectators applauded. Even the jurors, rather than feeling cheated of their role in the judicial process, believed the situation had led to a just verdict. An enterprising journalist later interviewed jurors and concluded that they favored an acquittal for Harry and Judd but leaned toward jail time for Deetie, whose sob story, while convincing and probably accurate, just did not justify Cook's slaying.[88]

Deetie continued to fascinate. A journalist watched her carefully as she stood to receive her sentence. "Garbed in a dark blue coat with a large mink collar and wearing a white turban hat, Marguerite stood erect before the bar to hear her fate."

Deetie, "who appeared years younger than yesterday when she collapsed after her mad hysteria," was all smiles.

She thanked the judge when he sentenced her to a term of three to fifteen years; "She again went to the arms of her mother but this time she did not cry. Both laughed gayly."[89]

Before deputies took her back to jail, Deetie posed for photographers.

After the trial, Deetie penned two additional poems, one of which was titled "Prison."

> You see gray walls of iron and stone
>   may hear a piteous cry or moan,
> You shudder and turn your eyes away,
>   The path of the sinner does not pay.
> But here, we know as we are known
>   Not by this shell of flesh and bone,
> For what we see in this strange place
>   Is neither poverty, color nor race,
> But hearts that are bared to our tearful gaze,
>   And when we find through the hours and days,
> Are hearts of courage, of kindness and love.
>   "Why! That must be what our Father above
> Meant when He said "I prepare you a home
>   "Where ye shall know as ye are known."

'Tis heaven to understand His Grace
The gray walls do not make this place
But aching hearts that are seeking peace
Content to wait for His release.[90]

Marguerite "Deetie" Bumbaugh served less than the minimum threshold of her sentence; after two years, five months and eighteen days, she left prison a free woman in November 1930. Prison officials cited her exemplary behavior as one of the reasons for her early release from the Detroit House of Correction.

Deetie returned to Indiana, where she married Herbert Ashton. The woman whose face sold a thousand newspapers died in Los Angeles County, California, on August 19, 1970, at the age of seventy-two.

5

THE "BABY MURDER FARM" CASE

EAU CLAIRE, 1929

Berrien County sheriff Fred G. Bryant and prosecuting attorney Wilbur N. Cunningham had never seen anything quite like it. A local newspaperman described the twisted, mind-bending tale as "one of the most weird and gruesome in the criminal annals of Berrien County."[91]

The character at the center of the "weird and gruesome" story was twenty-five-year-old Dowagiac resident Oakel Gorham.

Born Oakel Ford in 1904, she was the second wife of widower Herbert Gorham, a sixty-one-year-old foundry worker whose first wife, Lillie, died in 1919 of tuberculosis. When Gorham wed Oakel in 1922, she was eighteen and he was fifty-four and a father of ten from his first marriage. Oakel and Herbert had six children together, only two of whom lived past the age of two. In February 1929, the family of five—Herbert, Oakel and their children Hazel, Violet and Clarence—occupied a small house in Dowagiac.

Statements later made by Oakel suggested that Herbert Gorham had a drinking problem and sometimes wobbled home inebriated. Such instances created friction and led to heated arguments.

Oakel Gorham wasn't an unattractive woman. She wore her hair in a stylish bob, but she had a watcheye that made it difficult to determine where she was looking. Some said she had the mentality of an eight-year-old, and reporters regularly described her as a simpleton or feeble-minded. Herbert later described Oakel as a fantasist who "stretches the truth a lot sometimes."

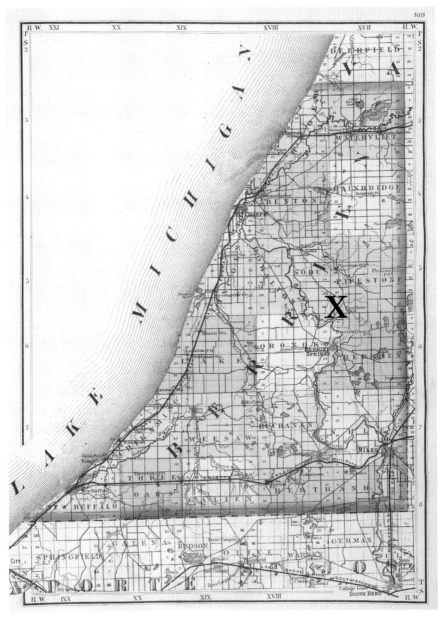

Above: Berrien County from the 1873 Walling Atlas. "X" marks the spot of the so-called Baby Murder Farm. *Original map from the University of Michigan Library.*

Opposite: Cass County from the 1873 Walling Atlas. "X" marks the spot where Oakel Gorham lived. On the day her son died, she carried him the distance due west from Dowagiac to Eau Claire (see Berrien County map). *Original map from the University of Michigan Library.*

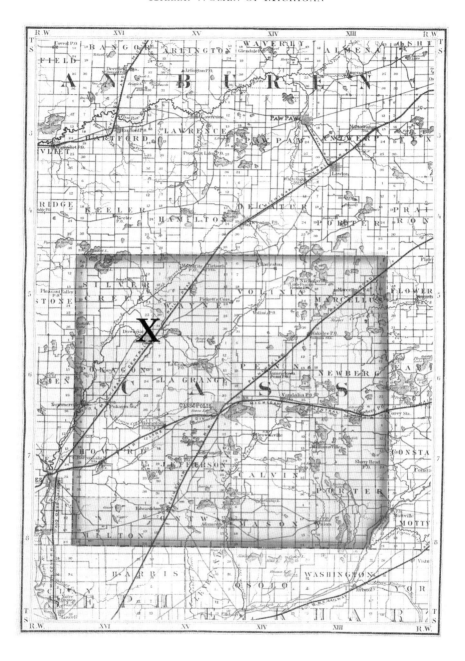

Herbert was a tall drink of water with a mop of sandy hair perched atop a stork-like neck. A myriad of wrinkles on the parchment-like skin of his face told of sixty hard years. There was no love lost between Oakel's elderly husband and her mother, Ethel, who was twelve years younger than her stepson. "Well, I warned her she'd have trouble if she married him," Ethel later recalled. "An old man like that, and he'd been married before and had children. I told Herb to leave her alone, but he wouldn't do it."[92]

Oakel's mother, the former wife of Big Rapids–area farmer Harry Ford, stood half a head taller than her second husband, Wallace "Shorty" Lewis. Ethel could usually be found wearing a once white flower-print dress that time had turned into a shade of light yellow, while her husband typically donned a pair of denim overalls streaked with dirt and grease. They lived with Ethel's two children—twelve-year-old Ransom and ten-year-old Charles—in a squalid three-room cabin on the edge of Eau Claire, a community of about three hundred residents in central Berrien County. Ransom, Ethel believed, was the product of a previous relationship with a lumberjack named Nathan Thurston. Charles was Harry Ford's boy.

Shorty Lewis supported his family by picking through garbage in the village dump, conveniently situated next to their house. Shorty and Ethel were hoarders; their property was a garden of half-buried objects such as old bottles that he had picked from the dump. They threw nothing away; stacks of yellowed newspaper stood in every corner of every room. The

Oakel Gorham, Herbert Gorham, Shorty Lewis and Ethel Lewis. *Author's collection.*

largest room of the house was stacked floor to ceiling with Shorty's pickings. The family of four lived in the other two rooms in a house with no running water and heat from a single pot-belly stove. Ethel was, like her daughter, considered slow-witted.

Mother and daughter quarreled often, according to Herbert Gorham, who admitted a disliking for his mother-in-law. "They had plenty of fights," he told a reporter. "I saw 'em tear into each other once, they knocked the table over."[93]

Despite occasional rows, Oakel and her mother remained close. Undeterred by the ten-mile distance, Oakel sometimes walked to her mother's shack barefooted and carrying a child swaddled in her arms.

The case began with the death of five-month-old Clarence Wesley Gorham on Sunday, February 10, 1929, at his grandmother's house in Eau Claire. According to Oakel, on the previous Thursday, Herbert came home drunk and, during a particularly nasty quarrel, sent his wife packing. She took their three children—Violet, Hazel and Clarence—and retreated to her mother's residence in Eau Claire. They made the ten-mile trek on foot, with Oakel carrying Clarence, who was swaddled in rags too thin to protect him from the biting wind. Herbert would later deny exiling his wife and said that she had taken the children, he did not know where, on Friday.

Around five o'clock on Sunday morning, Clarence died. The cause of death was ascribed to whooping cough, but those familiar with Oakel's history began to suspect foul play.[94] Clarence was the fourth Gorham child to pass away since 1923 and the third to die at their grandmother's house.

Louise May Gorham died on February 21, 1923, at just over a month old. Cass County coroner S.E. Bryant inked the cause of death as "malicious neglect in regard to feeding and care," but an inquiry by a one-man grand jury went nowhere.[95]

Nine-day-old Mary Jane died at the Gorham residence in Dowagiac on March 1, 1925, of "auto toxemia from acute indigestion."[96] Carrie Wallace, a boarder who lived with the family at the time, later said that the newborn died after Oakel pinched her in a fit of violence.

Three months later, Mary Jane's older sister, eighteen-month-old Isabelle May, died. The second Gorham child to die in the Lewis residence (following Louise May) raised eyebrows among the small farming community and bewildered Coroner S.E. Bryant, who scrawled, "This child died under suspicious circumstances," on Isabelle May's death certificate.[97] According to Herbert, he followed the undertaker's advice and had Isabelle's stomach sent to a chemist in Ann Arbor, but he did not have the one hundred dollars required to pay for the analysis.[98]

Following the untimely demise of Clarence, the fourth Gorham child to die before reaching the age of two, Bryant's suspicions of foul play deepened. He contacted Sheriff Fred G. Bryant, who brought Oakel and her mother in for questioning. He also "invited" their husbands along for the ride as potential witnesses of infanticide.

Berrien County prosecuting attorney Wilbur Cunningham and Deputies Charles Andrews and Ray Hall questioned the suspects together. They made a motley crew that police described as "sub normal."[99] Oakel sat facing her mother, whose crippled right arm dangled by her side. Shorty, whose oversized overalls and shoes gave him a clown-like appearance, sat next to Ethel. A reporter described him as "a little man weighing 98 pounds and less than four feet, 10 inches tall." Herbert Gorham completed the oddball quartet.

Words poured from Oakel's mouth like water from an open tap. Choking back tears, in a cracking squawk, she accused her mother of murdering Louise, Isabelle and Clarence.[100]

According to Oakel, her young stepbrother told her that "Ma"—Ethel Lewis—throttled Louise and later poisoned Isabelle.

"Were you there when Isabelle died?" Deputy Andrews asked. "How did she die?"

"She died right in my arms," Oakel replied.

"Who killed Isabelle?"

"Ma—I ain't telling a lie either."

"How was Isabelle killed?"

"She put dope in the milk."

Oakel offered a strange description of Isabelle's demise: "Her brains popped out."

"Oakel!" Ethel said, stomping her feet and stabbing the air with her index finger. "Oakel! You are lying. How can you say those things about your mother, after I have helped you, fed you and your babies and did so many things for you!"

"I'm telling the truth! I'm telling the truth!" Oakel responded with a singsong intonation a reporter described as a "chant." "I've got two more babies and I don't want to go to jail."[101]

Oakel also accused her mother of killing Clarence following a heated argument between mother and daughter over the cost of milk and the additional mouths she would have to feed. They discussed putting Clarence up for adoption, and at some point, Oakel said, her mother declared, "I'll help you get rid of one of them." Then Ethel took a bottle of amber-colored fluid from a kitchen cupboard and fed three doses of the "red dope" to Clarence.

"When I woke up in the morning the baby was gasping hard for breath," Oakel continued. "I laid it in its bed and dressed the other two children. Then I went back to Clarence. He was almost lifeless. He died in my arms. There was blood on the pillow and blood flowing from its mouth and nose."[102]

"Did you ask her to do it?" Andrews asked.

"No sir, I did not," Oakel insisted. "No sir, I did not. I didn't say anything about it."

Asked about her mother's motive for murdering the children, Oakel said, "She was mad because I came up there and visited. I thought it was alright. She got mad because I came."

"What made her kill Louise and Isabelle May?"

"She was edgeways at me."

"Did you ask her to do it?" Andrews repeated his earlier question.

"No I did not."

She did not, however, see "Ma" choke Clarence. Nevertheless, she explained, she knew that her mother had done it. "Sunday morning about 15 or 20 minutes after Ma choked him I saw finger prints on his throat and I know Ma did it because Ma acted funny and couldn't look me in the face. She was the only one around the baby. I picked him up and Pa says he's dead and she was the only one around the baby." Oakel added that "Ma" told her she was going to choke Clarence.

Oakel also said that her mother had disposed of four of her own children, including twins whom she buried behind the barn on the Ford farm near Big Rapids. Ethel Lewis, according to her daughter's statement, had killed seven children. Shorty admitted to burying two of the four but indicated that they were premature or stillborn.

Mecosta County sheriff Charles Kanehl condemned Oakel's story of the dead twins as an outright fabrication. "If Mrs. Lewis' daughter said her mother murdered two babies while the wife of Harry Ford of this city," he declared, "she is laboring under a delusion."[103] Ford also denied the tale but said that he believed his former wife to be capable of murder nonetheless.

Oakel's responses were jumbled, disconnected, disordered and contradictory. She confused dates and places. She said Louise died in 1927 when in fact her death occurred four years earlier. In one answer, she said her three children died in her mother's Eau Claire house; in another, she said they died at her home in Dowagiac. These inconsistencies led to doubts about the veracity of her statement and underscored growing concerns about Oakel's mental stability.

Ethel Lewis admitted to adding one drop of "sore mouth medicine" to the milk she gave Clarence. The baby did not have mouth sores, she said, but she always added the medicine—which was in a rose-colored or "pinkish" bottle—as a preventative measure. She repeatedly denied harming any of her grandchildren, but the wording of one particular denial was peculiar. "I didn't poison these children—I didn't choke them," she said. "I didn't know it would cause all this trouble. Other people have got rid of children, and nothing happened."[104]

The last statement rang like a partial confession, but when pressed, Ethel explained that she was referring to abortionists or doctors who performed "illegal surgeries."

Ethel offered a different version of the events leading up to Clarence's death during a later round of questioning by Wilbur Cunningham.

"When Oakel went to bed she said she ought to give it some milk," Ethel told Cunningham. "I said wait 'til it wakes up. It woke up around 1 or 2 o'clock in the morning. It was a rattlin' its throat. Its throat was filling up, and it went down on it. It was whooping cough."

"But the doctor says the baby didn't have the whooping cough," Cunningham noted.

"Well," Ethel shrugged, "it was a rattlin' in its throat anyway. Next mornin' Oakel said, 'Ma, what ails the baby?' I said I'd be there pretty soon, and that maybe it would be all right. She picked up the baby and shook it hard. It breathed two times."

"Now, why should Oakel say you killed the baby if she didn't know you did?"

"Bless your heart," Ethel responded, "I don't know."

Cunningham tried another tack. "What did you put aconite in the baby's milk for?"

Once again, Ethel denied any wrongdoing. "I didn't put aconite in the milk. It was sore mouth medicine I got from Dr. Hubbard."

"Why would Oakel say you killed her baby?"

"She wants to put me over the road so she can have what I've got in the house."

"Oakel doesn't tell lies, does she?" the prosecutor asked.

"Well, yes, sometimes she does."

"What have you got in the house that Oakel wants?"

"Oh, there are some things she wants to take home. I got some things hid away, so she can't find them. Some handkerchiefs and jack knives for the children, and things."

It seemed incredible that Oakel Gorham would accuse her mother of murdering children in order to obtain trinkets, but then stranger things have happened.

Cunningham's patience was growing thin. "Now listen here, Mrs. Lewis, who killed Clarence Wesley?"

"Goodness sakes, Mister, I don't know. Probably you think it's me? I didn't choke it, and I didn't poison it."

"Did you smother it?"

"No I didn't smother it."

Deputy David Tyner took over the questioning.

"A baby crying makes you nervous, doesn't it, Mrs. Lewis?"

"Yes it does," Ethel agreed. "It makes me quiver all inside. Sometimes I can't hardly stand it. It sets me crazy, and I don't know what I'm doing. Everything goes black before my eyes."

"The baby cried Saturday night, didn't it?" Tyner asked.

"Yes it did, quite a little."

"Don't you suppose you might have had one of those spells, and maybe reached out and put your hand over its mouth to shut off its crying?"

"I never touched the child," Ethel insisted. "Oakel put it to bed, Mister."[105]

Herbert Gorham stood by his young wife. "She [Ethel Lewis] must have done something," he told reporters. "I can't think of nothing else. Funny though, that three of them died at her place, when they were all right before."[106]

Cunningham heard enough to charge both women with first-degree murder. Sheriff Bryant released the men, but Oakel and her mother remained in the county jail while investigators searched for physical evidence verifying Oakel's allegations. Either poison found in Clarence'd internal organs or a bottle of "red dope" found at the Lewis residence could send both women to prison for life.

Despite the inconsistencies in Oakel's statement and Ethel's repeated denials, Oakel Gorham told a compelling story. Sheriff Bryant sent a crew to the Lewis residence to search for the mysterious rose-colored bottle in the hills of junk. A small legion of newspapermen descended on the dilapidated shack, which they christened the "Murder Farm."

One reporter described the scene. "The little structure that served as a home contains but two rooms and a large boarded-in porch at the rear, where piles and piles of buckets, old clothing, [a] harness, fruit jars and other unused articles are stacked to the five-foot ceiling."[107]

The family of four all slept in the same tiny room that Ethel had decorated by covering the walls with pictures torn out of magazines and mail-order catalogues.

A translucent white sheet of ice covered everything in the house, including a skeletal, half-frozen terrier lying inert on the floorboards of the bedroom.

While investigators combed the Eau Claire residence for the elusive bottle of "red dope," Cass County coroner S.E. Bryant and Berrien County coroner George Slaughter examined the body of Clarence Gorham at a Dowagiac undertaking establishment. Bryant did not find any evidence of physical trauma on the baby's neck: no bruising, no finger marks, no fractured hyoid bone—nothing to prove that Ethel Lewis had throttled Clarence as Oakel alleged. Bryant then prepared the body for shipment to Lansing for an in-depth post-mortem, including a chemical analysis of the stomach contents.

Back at the county jail, the two suspects prepared for their first day in court. "What does it mean to plead guilty?"

It was a child's question asked by a twenty-five-year-old woman as she prepared to leave the Berrien County Jail for the arraignment. Evidently, Oakel Gorham, who left the fourth grade at age twelve and never returned to a classroom, did not understand the legal whirlpool in which she was submerged.

On the morning of February 14, Sheriff Bryant brought the two suspects to court. Rather than the bedraggled appearance of a sleepless night, the women appeared refreshed.

That something was amiss in the minds of the two women became apparent when sheriff deputies escorted them to court for the arraignment on murder charges. Despite facing life in prison, the two women chatted amiably as if nothing had happened, as if daughter hadn't accused mother of cold-blooded murder and mother hadn't countered by accusing daughter of lying. "Nice out, ain't it?" Oakel remarked as she stepped outside for the first time since her arrest.[108]

The strange affect prompted one journalist to describe them as an "odd pair" and underscored the possibility that the women did not understand their precarious legal situation. "There is a possibility of the two women being given a mental test," noted a journalist about the growing concern for the sanity of Oakel and her mother. "Both are simple minded, officers state, with intellects of an eight-year-old child."[109]

"The murder warrants were read by the justice to the pitifully illiterate women," wrote a journalist who witnessed the arraignment of the accused baby-slayers. "It was plain they did not know what it was all about."

"I didn't kill it, I didn't kill it," Ethel exclaimed when she heard the charge. "No sir, no ma'am, I did not. I don't know anything about it."

Judge Elizabeth Forham ordered them held over to circuit court and returned to jail without bail.

The criminal case would hinge on the tests in Lansing. If Clarence's internal organs contained poison, the women would face a judge and jury. If the tests came back negative, they would face a panel of doctors; Sheriff Bryant vowed to have their sanity tested. The women probably did not understand or realize that one way or the other, their freedom had come to an end.

While Ethel whiled away the time in a Berrien County Jail cell, her two boys enjoyed what seemed like the high life in the county detention home. The half brothers reveled in a bathtub, soaking for a half an hour in the hot water. They wrote notes to their jailed mother and told shocking stories of their life in the Eau Claire shack.

The weekend that Clarence died, all eight family members—Ransom, Charlie, Ethel, Wallace, Oakel, Hazel, Violet and Clarence—slept in two beds in one room. "I slept with dad on the cot," Charlie explained to the house matron. "Mother, Oakel, and her three babies slept at the top of the larger bed (which is only three-quarter size) and Ransom slept at the foot. We heated large hunks of bark on the cook stove and would take them to bed to keep warm."[110]

The "Baby Murder Farm" headlines traveled across Michigan and inspired a draconian proposal to prevent the "insane, feeble-minded, idiots, imbeciles, moral degenerates and sexual perverts" from having children. Lawmakers in Lansing used the story as an exemplum for a sterilization law. With their mugs plastered over front pages, the four principals made compelling poster children for the bill. Five of Herbert's ten children from his first wife ended up in an orphanage; four of his six children with Oakel died before the age of two; and Ethel's two children lived in an unheated, uninsulated shack with a metal sheeting over the wall boards as the only protection from the elements.

The bill proposed to change an existing law that required the consent of the individual before a sterilization procedure. The new law would take away the individual's right of consent and replace it with a trial by jury in probate court. The twelve jurors would determine the necessity of mandatory sterilization.[111]

Although sterilization laws in other states were considered unconstitutional, Michigan legislators appeared ready to forge ahead despite the Supreme Court's rulings.

Meanwhile, the evidence supporting first-degree murder charges began to mount.

After hours of searching, the crew in Eau Claire found four bottles of interest. One, labeled "Sore Mouth Medicine," contained an amber-colored fluid. Oakel identified the bottle but claimed that the "medicine" Ethel fed Clarence was more reddish in color.

Another bottle contained aconite. Derived from a plant, the toxic substance was sometimes used as a sort of panacea to treat anything from diarrhea to heart disease. Oakel admitted taking aconite to calm her nerves.

The other two bottles contained triple bromide, a sedative often used by insomniacs and the nervous. One teaspoon would send an adult into a deep slumber but could kill a child. Police suspected that the "red dope" might have come from one of these two bottles, perhaps to help the baby sleep, but Ethel Lewis said she used the bromide for her heart.

Carrie Wallace, a one-time boarder at the Gorham house in Dowagiac, described an incident that appeared to support Ethel Lewis's statement about Oakel violently shaking Clarence before he died. According to Wallace, Oakel lost her temper, grabbed nine-day-old Mary Jane by the throat, shook her and pinched her in the stomach. The newborn died two days later.

Herbert did not help Oakel's case when he discussed the incident with a *News-Palladium* reporter. "Carrie and Jim Wallace, who were living with us then," he explained, "said Oakel choked it accidentally when she pushed it away from her. She must have hurt it, 'cause it wouldn't eat much after that. It had spasms."[112]

Oakel's accusations, on the other hand, did not stand up to scrutiny. She alleged that her mother throttled her twins in Big Rapids and even said she witnessed the murders in one rendition of the story, but both Ethel and her former husband Harry Ford insisted they never had twins.

Oakel alleged that her mother choked Clarence and that she saw the fingermarks encircling his throat, but doctors found no marks of violence on the infant.

Investigators began to suspect that the baby slayings took place nowhere but in the mind of Oakel Gorham.

The case was a gold mine for students of the human mind.

On Tuesday, February 19, 1929, William Roemer, a professor of psychiatry at the University of Notre Dame, made the trip north to meet with the enigmatic women at the heart of the weird case, not in any official capacity, but to study their mindset. After two hours with the suspected slayers, Professor Roemer concluded that they were fit to stand trial and that Oakel did not fabricate her accusations against her mother, although he added a caveat: "Of course, it is very possible her imagination is distorted for minute details."[113]

He considered both women sane but of "below normal" intelligence. Each understood right from wrong. "They understand questions asked of them," he added, "but, of course, they might be easily led to give answer[s] they would not intend to make." This latter observation applied to some of the more incriminating statements they made during their interrogations.

A full-page spread devoted to the case appeared in the Sunday, March 3 edition the *Detroit Free Press* titled "Michigan Baby Slaying Case Lacks Parallel." In it, journalist James M. Haswell contemplated the psychology behind the murders. Paying close attention to the statements of the two women, particularly Ethel's response to Deputy Tyner's questions about how a baby's crying sent her into a "spell," Haswell noted that "both mothers seem to have been subject to a curious lack of emotional control, a kind of fitful hysteria induced at times by the incessant demands that every infant makes. In short, neither woman could stand the babies' crying, and, if eventually the deaths be proved to have occurred as Oakel Gorham states, acted in a sort of frenzy of impatience to stop their wailings."[114]

A few days after Roemer's comments hit the front pages, Wilbur Cunningham asked Circuit Court judge Charles E. White to form a sanity commission to examine the defendants before they made their pleas in court. White appointed Drs. Roy A. Morter and C.N. Sowers. Dr. Morter worked for the State Hospital in Kalamazoo and was notable as the psychiatrist who examined Marguerite Bumbaugh to determine her fitness to stand trial after she gunned down her former boss, Niles manufacturer Walter Cook.

In a seven-hour marathon interview, the commissioners examined Oakel Gorham and Ethel Lewis in the county jail on Wednesday, March

6, and filed their report two days later. According to the report, Oakel had the mentality of a seven-year-old and suffered from delusions.

"She is very indifferent and unemotional and suggestible on all subjects except certain fixed ideas which she has regarding her mother's conduct toward her children and her mother's children," the report noted.

"These ideas show gross misinterpretation and are so illogical that we consider them delusions rather than fabrications. Her description regarding the details of her mother's abuses toward the children are contradictory. She does not realize the wrong done by making contradictory statements. She accuses her mother but has no knowledge of the consequences of her accusations."

"It is our opinion that she has a mind that never has developed beyond the seventh year level and she has superimposed upon this a mental deficiency which prevents her from distinguishing right from wrong, and renders her unable to foresee the consequences of an act." The commission recommended that Oakel Gorham be sterilized and sent to the State Hospital.

The report characterized Ethel Lewis as "truthful but primitive. She expresses no delusions. She makes no contradictory statements. There is no evidence of insanity." Although considered sane, Ethel Lewis possessed an even less well-developed intellect than her daughter. The commission indicated that she had the mentality of a six-and-a-half-year-old. They recommended sterilization and commitment to the Michigan Home and Training School for the Feeble-Minded in Lapeer.[115]

The commission's report ended the court case against both women. Because the defendants were unable to stand trial, the murder warrants were dismissed. By April, the women had been committed to their new homes: the State Hospital for Oakel and the Michigan Home and Training School for Ethel.

Because the Eau Claire "Baby Farm" case ended with the commitments of Oakel Gorham and Ethel Lewis instead of a trial, the cause of Clarence's demise is a question without a solid answer. There are, however, clues as to what might have happened.

The first clue can be found in the death records of the first and third Gorham child to pass away. When Louise Gorham died in 1923, Dr. S.E. Bryant described the infant's cause of death as "malicious neglect in regard to feeding and care." This finding must have triggered questions about Oakel's fitness as a parent because it led to a one-man grand jury.

Bryant's notation on Isabelle Gorham's death certificate—"This child died under suspicious circumstances"—illustrates the physician's growing concerns about neglect in the Gorham household.

The second clue is contained in the statement of Carrie Wallace, who claimed to have seen Oakel shaking nine-day-old Mary Jane by the neck and violently pinching her in the abdomen—an incident Herbert Gorham later verified.

The third clue comes from an unnamed neighbor who said that she saw Oakel and the children arriving at the Wallace cabin on foot. A ten-mile hike in the dead of winter with nothing but rags to cover Clarence was yet another example of the neglect that endangered Oakel's children. Not surprisingly, the tyke developed a cough that Ethel likened to "whooping cough."

The fourth clue comes from a statement Ethel made during her second interrogation. In defending herself from her daughter's accusations of murdering Clarence, she said that Oakel "picked up the baby and shook it hard. It breathed two times." This is consistent with what Carrie Wallace claimed to have seen prior to the demise of Mary Jane four years earlier.

These four clues suggest a pattern of abuse perpetrated by none other than Oakel Gorham. If the psychologists nailed their diagnosis of Oakel—that she was "unable to see the consequences of an act"—then she may have accidentally killed Clarence when she tried to quiet his wailing with a vigorous shaking, just as she may have accidentally killed Mary Jane and possibly Louise, although nothing in the historical record exists to substantiate Dr. Bryant's comment about "malicious neglect."

It is tempting to consider that Oakel, realizing another death would jeopardize her custody of the two remaining Gorham children, decided to pin the murder on her mother. The sanity commission's report, however, suggests that this degree of manipulation was simply beyond her comprehension.

More likely, she shook Clarence without realizing that it could kill him. The next morning, when Clarence died, she remembered seeing her mother feeding him a bottle of milk. Believing that her mother murdered her own twins years earlier in Big Rapids, she came to believe that Ethel poisoned Clarence.

Ethel Lewis died in 1956 at the age of seventy-four. Her obituary in the *Herald-Palladium* did not mention her connection to one of Berrien County's most spectacular and bizarre criminal cases.[116]

Oakel Gorham spent several decades in the State Hospital in Kalamazoo. She was dangerous to her children, to her mother and to police. That she did not realize she was dangerous made her even more so.

6

THE HEIRESS AND THE MECHANIC

FLINT, 1932

Helen Joy Morgan repeatedly lied about her age. When she became a press darling in 1931, she repeatedly reduced her age by over a decade by telling both police and pressmen that she was twenty-seven. Something about her true age must have horrified her, which hints at the vanity that in part may have motivated the murder of Leslie Casteel.

If the prosecution's theory of the crime was accurate, then Morgan's choice of a cemetery for the murder of her paramour may have been an indication of her mindset. Concluding that her storybook romance had come to an end, she decided to bury her Prince Charming.

They came from opposite worlds.

Forty-year-old Helen Joy Morgan was the only child of Edward and Carrie Morgan.[117] A real estate mogul, Edward had accumulated a portfolio that included several valuable properties in the Chicago Loop. The family's real estate holdings grew to include properties in Flint, Michigan, as well as an eighty-three-acre spread near Pasadena, California. As heiress to a considerable fortune, Helen grew up alongside the daughters of Chicago's social elite. She attended Chicago's Englewood High School and later the Morris Academy, a prestigious finishing school in Morris, Illinois.

In the early 1920s, Helen moved with her mother to Flint, where she delighted in taking long drives through the countryside in her REO sedan.

She was not an unattractive woman. High-arched eyebrows, a pie-shaped face and narrow lips gave her a Betty Boop–like appearance. Although Helen

Joy Morgan maintained this girl-next-door appearance and hourglass figure in her middle-age years, she later described herself as a sort of wallflower who did not know love until she met the man of her dreams—a mechanic named Leslie Casteel.

With chiseled features and the physique of a wrestler, Leslie Casteel had no trouble finding romantic partners, but he also had a bit of a zipper problem. When he met Helen Joy Morgan, Casteel had notched innumerable relationships, including three failed marriages.

A native of West Virginia, Casteel came north sometime in the mid-twenties. He settled in Flint, where he worked as an auto mechanic.

Their twisted fairy-tale romance began one sunny spring day when Morgan's REO sedan broke down, an incident that brought her face-to-face with Casteel.

The heiress may have been just another conquest for Casteel, but Morgan was smitten. They began a torrid affair that irked Helen's elderly mother, Carrie, who berated her daughter for seeing someone from the other side of the tracks, scorned the idea of a marriage, forbid Casteel from ever stepping onto her property and threatened to cut off Helen if she persisted. It was no empty threat. The Morgan matriarch changed her will and disinherited her only child to prevent Casteel, whom Carrie despised, from enjoying so much as a red cent from the Morgan estate.

According to Casteel's sister Minnie Spiker, Carrie Morgan's threats transcended the family's finances. During her turn on the witness stand, Minnie related a conversation she had with Leslie about the threat. "Leslie asked me if I had heard about old Mrs. Morgan threatening him and I said no. He said she had threatened to shoot him if he came near her house."

Minnie asked Leslie if there was something he could do about the threat, but Helen spoke for him. "No," Helen responded, "my mother's money has too much influence over the law."

Spiker also said that at one time, Helen Morgan made this ominous statement: "If I don't live with Leslie Casteel, no one else will."[118]

Mason Simes, a coworker and friend of the Casteel family, later described a curious incident that appeared to underscore Helen Joy Morgan's subtle threat. One day while Casteel and Simes were working on a car, Morgan came into the garage. She palmed a .32 she had in her pocket and told Casteel to sit down. He smiled, as if he thought she was teasing, and sat in a chair as commanded. Then Morgan ordered Simes to leave, which he did.[119]

In the mind of Helen Joy Morgan, she and Leslie Casteel were married even though she did not have the certificate to prove it. And she was a jealous

Heiress turned murderess Helen Joy Morgan in a press photo from 1928. *Library of Congress.*

spouse. When Helen Singer, a childhood friend and laundress, came by Casteel's house to pick up a load of laundry one night, Morgan became suspicious. It was around nine o'clock in the evening—a little late for such a house call, Helen thought. Singer later relayed the anecdote in court.

"Who is this lady?" Morgan asked Casteel. He explained.

"Well, she'll have to go," Morgan responded.

"Then she turned to me and told me to get out and never come back or she would get the police after me," Singer said. "I said, 'Who are you?' and she said, 'I am his wife.'"[120]

To the delight of Carrie Morgan, the eternal flame of the relationship began to flicker. After two years of seeing Helen, Casteel turned his attention to other women.

Helen Joy Morgan was crushed. Although she had attracted the eye of a California restaurateur, to whom she became engaged, she still loved Casteel and just could not let go. Desperate to hold on to the mechanic, she threatened to kill him if he did not stop seeing other women. One of Casteel's lady friends, whom he dated throughout 1931, later told police that Helen's threats caused him to break off their relationship in January 1932. "He told me," she said, "he was afraid for both of us."[121]

When Casteel's house burned to the ground in February 1931, police suspected arson and questioned both Casteel and Morgan. When they were interviewed separately, the incident led to a sort of prisoner's dilemma. According to Morgan, she said nothing to incriminate Casteel, but nevertheless, he began to doubt her sincerity. Testimony at Morgan's murder trial indicated that Casteel's suspicions were not unfounded, that Helen Joy Morgan had in fact told authorities that Casteel had torched his own abode.

By the spring of 1931, Casteel felt like a caged animal. It became clear that he could only be free if he left Flint and Helen Joy Morgan behind him.

On the evening of April 23, 1931, the two ex-lovers met at the corner of Stone Street and Third Avenue, where Morgan picked up Casteel in her car. According to Morgan, Casteel arranged the meeting because he had learned that she planned on talking to the prosecutor, he surmised, to accuse him of arson. He was also steamed about Helen's relationship with the California restaurant owner.

As soon as Casteel hopped into Helen's car, he began to berate her for turning "stool pigeon." She drove him to a remote spot near the Glenwood Cemetery and parked the car. At this point, she later told police, he became violent. As she attempted to flee the vehicle, Casteel pulled a revolver from his pocket and threatened to shoot her. She grabbed the gun and managed to wrench it from Casteel's grip, but it went off during the struggle, one bullet piercing his heart and another tearing through his liver. Morgan pulled Casteel from the car, jumped back behind the wheel and raced home to her mother.

Nelson Roome was picking dandelions in the cemetery when he heard the shots. He watched as Morgan dragged Casteel from the car, lay him face up on the ground and stood over him for a few seconds. Then, Roome said, she climbed back into the car and sped away.

Morgan went straight to her mother's home, where she called Edward Buhler, a family friend and a real estate agent, to ask his advice.

"Have you had a fight? Buhler asked.

"Worse than that."

"Did you knock him down?"

"Worse than that."

"Did you shoot him?"

"Yes."

"Did you kill him?"

"No, I don't think so."

Buhler suggested Helen call the police. Inspector of Detectives Lowell Burke arrived at the Morgan home about thirty minutes after the shooting and escorted Helen Joy Morgan to police headquarters.

Seemingly unfazed by the possibility of a first-degree murder charge, she admitted to shooting Casteel but insisted it was in self-defense.

In this press photograph, "A" marks the spot where Helen Joy Morgan shot, and then dumped, Leslie Casteel. *Author's collection.*

Morgan's story of self-defense, however, contained holes. It seemed illogical that the 130-pound heiress could possibly overpower Casteel, who tipped the scales at about 240. Harold T. Gray, a former coworker, later described Casteel as "very close to perfect in strength and health." Gray told an interesting anecdote to illustrate Leslie Casteel's physical power: "I have seen him pick up the front wheel on an Essex automobile, standing on his toes, at the garage, just as a demonstration of his strength."[122]

It seemed equally illogical that the gun went off no fewer than five times during the struggle. Then there was the gun, which Morgan said belonged to Casteel. Investigation revealed that Casteel had purchased the automatic from a former coworker, but three separate eyewitnesses said they saw Morgan in possession of a .32 months before Casteel's killing. The previous January, she brought the handgun to a local hardware store to purchase bullets.

A possible motive surfaced when investigators learned that Casteel was about to leave Flint. These facts led to a scenario in which the jilted woman lured her lover to a remote area, where she brought a permanent end to his philandering with two slugs from a .32.

Unconvinced by Morgan's self-defense plea, prosecuting attorney Ralph M. Freeman decided to charge the heiress with premeditated murder. The court remanded Morgan to the county jail pending her trial, set to begin the following May.

The ordeal did not appear to bother Helen Joy Morgan, who assumed a stoic façade as she moved through the judicial process, but it unhinged her mother. Carrie Morgan wore a heavy white veil to shield her face from newspaper photographers and hide the dark circles that told of sleepless nights tossing and turning with worry about her only daughter's legal troubles. "She appeared to be on the verge of collapse and leaned heavily on the arm of a young woman companion, while entering and leaving the building," noted a *Flint Daily Journal* reporter, who spied her at the police headquarters.[123] After a brief meeting with Helen and her attorneys, Carrie Morgan's legs gave out; she had to be carried to a car and driven home.

Carrie Morgan hired the best available attorneys in an attempt to keep her daughter out of the Detroit House of Correction. The trial, which captivated headlines for about a week in mid-January 1932, became a standing-room-only sensation. Arguing for the people, Ralph Freeman had little trouble placing the .32 automatic in the hand of Helen Joy Morgan. Through a series of witnesses that included Casteel's friends, family and coworkers,

Freeman also succeeded in depicting the defendant as a jealous, obsessive woman who stalked her ex-lover and used a .32 to end his womanizing and thus ensure his eternal devotion.

One witness, an employee of a hardware store where Morgan purchased bullets for the .32, relayed an interesting conversation he had with the accused a few weeks before the murder. Helen Joy Morgan told him that she was deeply in love with a man who had been thrice divorced. She then asked the clerk if such a man could be reformed. He replied, "Yes, there is always a chance. God can clean up any man."[124]

Morgan's team of attorneys, led by John H. Farley, did their best to put the .32 automatic in the hands of Leslie Casteel. One eyewitness told of Casteel taking the gun from a dresser drawer and showing it to him just a few weeks before the murder. To counter the testimony of the hardware store clerk, the defense attempted to show that Casteel sent Helen to purchase bullets for his .32 because, he believed, with his shady past and former legal troubles, he would not be able to obtain the ammunition himself. The defense also presented testimony to the effect that Helen Morgan did not know how to fire the gun and lacked the physical strength needed to cock the weapon.

The defense, however, decided not to put Morgan on the stand, so the jurors went into deliberations without hearing a word from the accused.

Instead, they had to settle for the closing comments of Morgan's defense, who attempted to char Casteel by depicting him as a good-for-nothing womanizer with an overactive libido. Farley declared his client "had the right to shoot Leslie Casteel down like a dog—she shot only in self-defense and that is the only defense in this case."[125]

In Farley's closing, Helen Joy Morgan became a heroic woman who resisted her mother's attempts to save her from a disastrous relationship—a conflict that led to a rift between mother and daughter. All for the love of a man who viewed Helen Joy Morgan as just another notch in his belt. In this imagining of the crime, she became the victim and the victim the perpetrator.

Helen kept her composure throughout the trial, but when Freeman skewered her self-defense story during his closing remarks, she stood from her chair and declared, "That's not true and you know it's not."[126]

The attempt to depict Casteel as the perpetrator amounted to a postmortem character assassination, which Judge Parker addressed in his instructions to the jury.

"There have been some statements made as to the character of Leslie Casteel," Parker noted. "He is dead and cannot come to this court to testify.

So far as the law is concerned, it makes no distinction between men. Human life is as sacred to the sweeper of the streets of Flint as it is to the President of the United States. No man has more right to take the life of the lowest than of the highest."[127]

Both Helen and Carrie Morgan remained impassive when the all-male jury returned a verdict of guilty of second-degree murder, which meant that the heiress would avoid a mandatory life sentence. The verdict of second-degree rather than first-degree murder indicated that the twelve men did not find conclusive evidence of premeditation, that, in mob parlance, she took Leslie Casteel for a ride.[128]

She maintained her stony countenance when Judge James S. Parker asked, "Have you anything to say why the sentence of the court should not be pronounced against you?"

"I have," Helen said. "I think I have had a most unfair trial. I am the victim of politics on the police department, and of the underworld. I am as innocent as anyone in this courtroom."[129]

Before the gavel dropped, ending the eight-day Helen Joy Morgan murder trial, the judge proclaimed the trial fair and the counsel adequate. Then he explained that although the second-degree murder conviction granted him the authority to send the now-convicted slayer to prison for life, he had decided on a lesser sentence of twenty to twenty-five years and would recommend the minimum of twenty.

Carrie Morgan wrapped her arms around Helen. "Don't worry, my child," a reporter heard her say, "mother will take care of you."[130]

After the verdict, Carrie Morgan cried foul and alleged that witnesses who would have proven her daughter's innocence were not allowed to testify. She vowed to continue the fight and guaranteed a retrial.

The entire front page of the *Flint Daily Journal*'s January 14, 1932 edition was devoted to the case. The headline "Miss Morgan Convicted," in massive type and all caps, stretched from margin to margin. To emphasize the golden spoon angle of the crime—a rich girl who did not get her way—the subtitle referred to Helen Joy Morgan by the epithet "Heiress," as *Daily Journal* writers had done throughout their reporting of the story.

Helen Joy Morgan briefly regained her freedom on bond as the Michigan Supreme Court considered her case, but when it affirmed the conviction, she returned for the remainder of her sentence in the Detroit House of Correction in Plymouth, Michigan.

The ordeal nearly broke Carrie Morgan. The high cost of Helen's defense depleted her fortune and sapped her strength. Cervical cancer

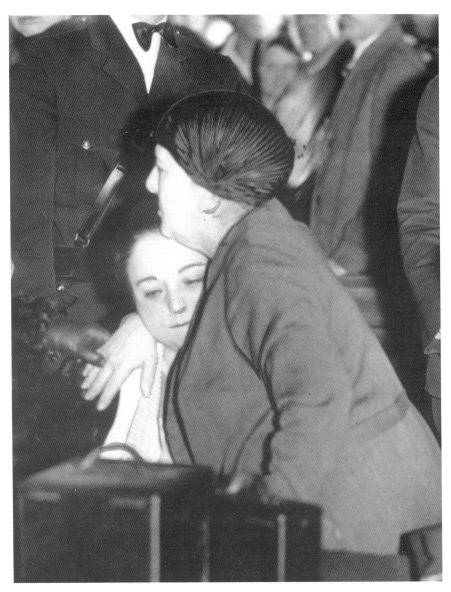

The Helen Joy Morgan murder trial captivated headlines and became big tabloid news. The *Detroit Mirror*, a short-lived tabloid, sent a photographer to Flint, where he snapped a photograph of the infamous defendant (*center*) and her mother, Carrie P. Morgan (*right*), just after the verdict. Carrie Morgan vowed to spend her last penny for her daughter's appeal. *Author's collection.*

further reduced the one-time juggernaut to skin and bones.[131] She died on September 6, 1934, at the age of sixty-two. For a second time, Helen Joy Morgan enjoyed a foray out of confinement when prison authorities allowed her to attend the funeral.

A model prisoner, Helen Joy Morgan left the Detroit House of Correction on parole in January 1943, her twenty-year sentence reduced to eleven years due to her good behavior and the goodwill of the parole board.

7
ALL IN THE FAMILY
CHEBOYGAN, 1932

Darius Lambert's kerosene lantern cut a swath through the inky black night as he stepped down the road toward his older brother Albert's cabin. Darius knew the "butter run" like the back of his hand. Albert Lambert, a fifty-four-year-old widower, lived about half a mile away on Grant Siding Road in Aloha Township.[132]

Darius; his forty-year-old wife, Minnie; and their ten children lived in a one-room house on a small farm about two miles west of Black Lake and a short walk to Albert's house. The geographic proximity was convenient for both brothers and led to an ongoing system of barter that would lead to the fateful butter run. Minnie churned Albert's butter in exchange for a portion of the product. Around 10:30 p.m. on Monday, August 1, 1932, Minnie sent Darius to fetch some butter.

The twelve Lamberts lived in a small one-room house that became a kiln on a hot day. The evening of August 1 was hot and sticky, so three of the Lambert boys—sixteen-year-old Harry, fourteen-year-old Raymond and twelve-year-old Russell—spent the night in a car parked on the property. Sometime around 10:30 p.m., they noticed their father headed down the road with a lantern in one hand and an empty butter crock tucked under his arm. The boys yelled "Pa," but Darius did not hear them and kept walking. A few minutes later, the cacophony of crickets and cicadas was interrupted by the crack of a gunshot.

On hearing the loud boom, Minnie darted out of the house and joined the boys by the car. According to Harry, she exclaimed, "Oh, my God. I'm

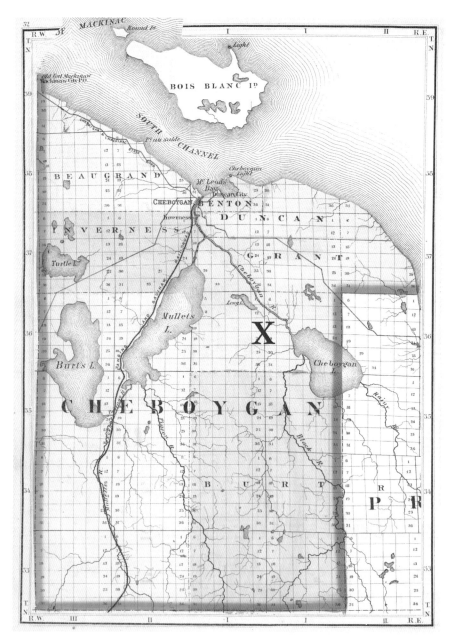

Cheboygan County from the 1873 Walling Atlas. "X" marks the spot of Darius Lambert's last milk run. Note: at the time the map was drawn, Black Lake was called Cheboygan Lake. *Original map from the University of Michigan Library.*

frightened!" After staring into the dark abyss for a few seconds, she returned to the house. Then the boys heard a second gunshot coming from the direction of Uncle Albert's residence.[133]

The fifteen-year-old son of a neighboring farmer, George Ketchabau Jr., had just returned home when he heard the gunshot followed by a voice exclaiming, "What are you shooting at?" The teenager later recalled that after hearing the first shot, he spotted the silhouette of a man carrying a lantern pass by the house. He watched as the figure continued down the road and disappeared from sight. A few seconds later, he heard a second gunshot.

If the silhouette belonged to Darius Lambert, then the youngster was the last person to see him alive.

About thirty minutes later, George Stokes—a farmer returning from visiting a friend—stumbled on Darius Lambert's body lying in the road. In his testimony at the coroner's inquest the following morning, Stokes recalled the horrific sight that materialized from the dark when he struck a match: Darius Lambert lying in a pool of warm blood, a gaping wound in his neck and his burnt overalls hanging from his arms and legs in charred strips. The pungent odor of burned flesh was overwhelming.

Stokes knelt down and tried to rouse Darius by shouting his name and shaking him. Unable to wake the dead, Stokes darted to the nearby residence of George Ketchabau. After relating his find, Stokes led his shocked neighbor to the grisly scene. Ketchabau took one glance at Lambert's smoldering remains and suggested they call Cheboygan County sheriff Charles Gilpin.

Gilpin arrived on the spot at approximately 1:00 a.m. on Tuesday, August 2. A cursory look indicated that someone had bushwhacked Lambert. Leaving the body in situ, he left to call Coroner W.E. Chapman, Dr. F.C. Mayne and state police lieutenant George Aldrich, and the group returned to analyze the crime scene.

A cluster of shot had shredded the side of Lambert's neck. The upward angle of the entrance wounds suggested that the perpetrator had fired from a crouching position approximately ten feet away. Darius's clothes had burned away, exposing portions of blackened flesh. The charred skeleton of a kerosene lantern next to his body suggested that when he collapsed to the ground, the lantern fell on top of him. The bowl broke, splashing kerosene that the flame ignited. Dr. Mayne would later say that if Lambert had not exsanguinated, he would have burned to death. His clothes were still smoldering when Mayne knelt down and examined the body.

Gilpin and Aldrich spent most of the morning interviewing friends and neighbors in the Black River area in an attempt to identify who may have pulled the trigger that widowed Minnie Lambert. By all accounts, Darius Lambert was a well-liked character who often helped out neighboring farmers. Minnie said she did not believe her husband had a single enemy in the world.

Then the two investigators learned that Albert and his sister-in-law had become a little too fond of each other. Local gossips told of a long-standing affair between Minnie and the elder Lambert brother.

Sixteen-year-old Harry Lambert told Gilpin and Aldrich that his mother spent around three hours every day at Uncle Albert's house. Sometimes, she would bring some of the kids, but as soon as they arrived, their uncle sent them on errands, ensuring that he would be alone with their mother. All three boys recalled one incident when their mother and father had words about Minnie's relationship with Albert. During the argument, Minnie stomped off and went straight to Albert's house.

This information suggested a possible scenario in which Minnie and Albert concocted a plan to do away with Darius so they could bring their relationship into the open, into a chapel where Mrs. Darius Lambert would become Mrs. Albert Lambert. At a predetermined time, Minnie would send Darius on the butter run (detectives found an empty crock next to his corpse), while Albert lay in wait somewhere along the way.

Gilpin and Aldrich searched Albert Lambert's home, where they found what they believed to be the smoking shotgun. Lambert owned four firearms—three shotguns and one rifle—that he said he had not used in a coon's age. A fine coat of dust covered all of the weapons except one of the shotguns, which appeared to have been recently fired; a faint scent of gunpowder lingered in the barrels. A smudge of still-damp blood on the trigger guard tied the gun to Albert, who had a cut on the webbing between his thumb and forefinger. Unable to provide an alibi for the time of the shooting, Albert Lambert was taken to the county jail for further questioning.

As Gilpin and Aldrich grilled Albert at the county jail, a curious scene occurred inside the Kimberly Undertaking Parlor, where Coroner W.E. Chapman convened a coroner's jury. The six men of the jury viewed Darius's body and then listened as county prosecutor James F. Shepherd questioned witnesses.[134]

Dr. Mayne described the effect of a shotgun on a human body at close range. The cluster of shot tore a gaping hole of three-inch diameter—larger than a silver dollar—in Darius Lambert's neck. The pellets had blown away a chunk of skin and the underlying muscle and opened the carotid artery. He died within seconds, as the arterial spray ebbed to a trickle and eventually ceased when his heart stopped.

With the dead body of their father lying on a table in an adjacent room, three of Darius's sons—Harry, Raymond and Russell—characterized their uncle's behavior toward their mother as a little too close for comfort. Their mother and uncle openly flirted with each other. Darius grumbled about his brother's attention to Minnie, and vice versa, but did not want to confront Albert. He did, the boys said, upbraid Minnie for her behavior.

The boys described visits to Uncle Albert's house when Albert would send them on errands, leaving him alone with Minnie for hours at time. They also related an incident when Minnie went for a drive with Albert, but Darius found out about it. He hopped in the back seat of the car and chided them for not inviting him along.

Minnie denied everything. She did not flirt with Albert, who never— not even once—sent the children away so they could enjoy some alone time. She emphatically denied knowing that Darius's butter run would be his last.

The jurors concluded that Darius had been murdered but did not have enough evidence to put the gun in Albert's hands. Nevertheless, the testimony persuaded Shepherd, who planned to prosecute Albert for first-degree murder. Justice Frank DeGowin made it official on Friday, August 5, when he signed a warrant charging Albert with fratricide.

Gilpin and Aldrich had handed Shepherd an air-tight case against Albert Lambert: a convincing piece of physical evidence—the shotgun— and a compelling motive. It was an age-old story with a predictable ending. Apart for some interesting hearsay, he did not have much of a case against Minnie Lambert, but that would change when Albert had a change of heart.

Faced with insurmountable evidence, Albert confessed to Sheriff Gilpin and Lieutenant Aldrich. In response to their questions, he detailed a plot to kill Darius Lambert. He pulled the trigger, he admitted, but Minnie planned it.

The previous spring—sometime in April—she handed him some shotgun shells and ordered him to "dispose" of her husband. When Albert failed to dispose of his brother, Minnie hounded him. Every few days, she would ask Albert when he planned to use the shotgun shells.

Albert resisted and told Minnie that he "didn't have the nerve," but Minnie eventually wore him down with her incessant harping. On the night of August 1, she sent Darius to his death.

Tiptoeing up behind his brother, Albert fired his first cluster. The first salvo of BBs flew over Darius's head.[135] This was the first shot heard by the Lambert boys and George Ketchabau Jr.

Darius paused, turned and yelled, "Whoever is doing that shooting better be careful!" He then continued toward Albert's house.

Albert crept farther down the road, knelt and aimed at the approaching silhouette.

"Did you shoot at his head?" Aldrich asked.

"I shot at his neck," Albert responded.[136]

The two officers drove Albert to the scene of the crime, where he guided them step-by-step through the entire episode.

In the confession, Albert cast Minnie as a malignant puppeteer hell-bent on her husband's demise. His admissions put her in jeopardy of a first-degree murder charge and a possible life sentence. Yet his confession raised a perplexing question: why the urgency to "dispose" of Darius?

Minnie would provide an eyebrow-raising answer to that question when she returned from Elberta, where she buried her husband's remains.

On Saturday night, August 6, Gilpin and Aldrich arrested Minnie Lambert. Backed into a corner by her lover's confession, Minnie admitted plotting Darius's murder. She and Albert tried to conceal their affair, which had been ongoing for several years, but somehow Darius suspected and threatened to kill Albert and banish her if he ever found proof.

Their clandestine affair continued hot and heavy through the spring and summer of 1931. Minnie managed to hide the smoking-gun evidence of their tryst by wearing larger and baggier clothes. Sooner or later, Darius would notice the pregnancy and thus find the proof that would doom the lovers.[137]

Afraid of losing both Albert and her children, Minnie plotted the murder and sent Darius on one final butter run.

The confessions brought a swift ending to the case that shocked northern Michigan's farming communities. About a week after Darius's murder, the two lovebirds stood in front of Judge Victor D. Sprague to receive their sentences.

A local reporter described the confessed-slayers. "She wore black dress under a light weight black coat. Her feet were in slippers. She is a small woman and walks with a slight limp. She is hard of hearing."

Even in court, Albert continued to fawn over Minnie. "He was constantly attentive to her," noted a *Cheboygan Daily Tribune* reporter. "He edged his chair closer to her side, and rested his arm on the arm of her chair. He picked two threads off her coat."[138]

Following a brief hearing, during which Shepherd called three witnesses in an attempt to fix the extent of blame—Dr. Mayne, Sheriff Gilpin and Lieutenant Aldrich—Judge Sprague sentenced both to life in prison at hard labor.

Minnie Lambert celebrated her forty-first birthday by taking one last automobile ride with Albert. At five thirty on the morning of Wednesday, August 10, the two now-convicted slayers left the county jail together and climbed into the back seat of a car driven by Charles Gilpin. Gilpin's wife, Mattie, and Deputy John Dalton completed the entourage. As the sun rose, the two ill-fated lovers motored south to begin their new life apart: she, in the Detroit House of Correction, and he in the State Prison at Jackson.

They would never see each other again. Albert Lambert, prisoner no. 32342, died of heart failure on August 29, 1944, at the age of sixty-six.[139]

Despite the *Cheboygan Daily Tribune* reporter's description ("She is a small woman"), Minnie Lambert was no skinny Minnie. She stood five-foot-six and tipped the scales at 220 when she entered the prison in 1932.

When Governor G. Mennen Williams commuted her sentence in 1950, cancer had reduced Minnie to less than half of her former self. She weighed a waifish eighty pounds when she left the Detroit House of Correction after serving eighteen years of her life sentence.

She planned to spend the remainder of her days, which doctors estimated to be no more than ten, with family in Flint. Doctors feared that the frail woman would die en route, but she arrived safely and exceeded the bleak ten-day estimate by several weeks.

The mother of ten and grandmother of thirty died on May 11, 1950, at the age of fifty-nine.

8

CHEMICAL DIVORCE

BARAGA, 1932

Being married to Elizabeth Ziolkowski was not a healthy proposition. By the fall of 1932, she had divorced one husband and buried two others. It was the unexpected demise of husband no. 3, John Ziolkowski, that etched her name on the list of Michigan's most dangerous women.

The daughter of Mitchell Clark and Madeline Busnow, Elizabeth grew up on a Chippewa Indian Reservation in Garden City, Ontario, Canada. The Clarks moved to the western Upper Peninsula of Michigan around 1890 when Elizabeth was fourteen years old. At age fifteen, she married twenty-three-year-old Oliver Moreau (Morrow).[140] They had eight children together during a twenty-year marriage that ended in divorce because of Moreau's heavy drinking. Although illiterate, Elizabeth had become a skilled seamstress.

In 1920, the forty-four-year-old married thirty-two-year-old John Boston, a World War I veteran and laborer at a Ford automotive plant in L'Anse. When Boston, an avid outdoorsman, returned home from an afternoon of ice fishing in 1932, Elizabeth served him a hot drink. Then she left to go shopping. When she returned, she found him dead. Elizabeth used a portion of the $1,800 life insurance money to purchase a house in Baraga and new car.

Seven months after the death of no. 2, the fifty-two-year-old grandmother married thirty-two-year-old John Ziolkowski, the son of a local farmer.[141]

In August, Elizabeth and John traversed the Upper Peninsula to spend some time with family in Fairport, a small fishing community nestled along the southern edge of the Garden Peninsula in Delta County. Their trip was cut short after only a few days because John became sick. He died a few weeks later after suffering from crippling convulsions that mystified Dr. H.J. Winkler and caused him to suspect a heavy metal poison. Winker's suspicions became fact when an autopsy revealed arsenic in John Ziolkowski's system.

Convinced that the elderly three-time widow dispatched John Ziolkowski to cash in on his life insurance, prosecutor Leo J. Brennan charged her with first-degree murder. County sheriff William A. Netti arrested her on October 5.

Lodged in a cell at the county jail, Elizabeth gave two separate statements to state police detective Fred Ennis in which she detailed her third husband's death after quaffing drinks she admitted to spiking with arsenic. The statements amounted to less than the confession that authorities wanted, however; the widow said that her husband asked her to give him the poison.

Since the suspect could neither read nor write, the written statement was stitched together from what she allegedly said to Ennis, which ended up verbatim in the *L'Anse Sentinel*'s October 13 edition:

> *About the middle of last August my husband and I motored to Fairport for a week's visit. John had been ill for two weeks with stomach trouble and, not improving, we returned after two days' visit. On our return he did not improve and the pains in his stomach seemed to get worse. On the second day after our return John asked me to get some arsenate of lead on a shelf in the shed and mix him a drink. He said it helped his stomach and seemed to ease the pain.*
>
> *I then said, "Why, John, have you been drinking that stuff?" but he did not answer. Then I asked him how it tasted and he said it was tasteless.*
>
> *To please my husband and to help ease his pains, I went into the shed and got some arsenate of lead, about as much as can be laid on a dime, mixed it with a glass of water and handed it to him. The poison made the water a milky color. After I gave this to John he drank it. This was shortly before noon and it seemed to make him feel better. He said he did not have any pains in his stomach and he got up and ate dinner with me.*
>
> *John seemed to feel better the rest of the day, but he did not eat a very large supper. John forbid me to tell this to any one and he even refused me to get him a doctor.*[142]

She added that, at John's request, she gave him a second dose two days later.

While Elizabeth said that she simply followed her husband's directions, she admitted to serving him a fatal dose of arsenic. Authorities began to wonder if she had poisoned her husband to collect a substantial $2,500 life insurance policy, which raised questions about John Boston's death four years earlier.

The similarities between Elizabeth's second and third husbands were hard to ignore. Both were World War I veterans. Both carried substantial life insurance policies. Both died premature deaths after drinking beverages served by Elizabeth.

In early November, a crew exhumed Boston's body, removed his stomach and intestines and sent them to a state chemist in Lansing, who discovered a large amount of arsenic.

Now suspected as a black widow, Elizabeth made a third statement in which she admitted to poisoning Ziolkowski not for his life insurance but because he had paid a little too much attention to her granddaughter. She also alleged that during a recent trip to New York, John had contracted a social disease.

"I gave my husband this poison," she added, "because I figured by getting rid of him I would also be rid of the other Ziolkowskis," whom she said were always poking their noses in her affairs.[143]

This new, revised statement painted the deceased as a pedophile and an adulterer, but the prosecuting attorney just could not move past that hefty life insurance policy. Elizabeth Ziolkowski was headed to trial, scheduled for January 1933.

The trial ended before it began when the accused slayer pleaded guilty. Judge John G. Stone sentenced her to life at hard labor.

A *L'Anse Sentinel* journalist watched the curious figure as she stood and received her sentence. "During the three months she has been confined in the County Jail she has aged greatly and the thoughts of what the future held in store for her no doubt undermined her health as she appeared frail and weary yesterday when she was brought into court."

The unnamed writer described Ziolkowski's crime as "fiendish and brutal and the product of a diseased mind. Her cruelty and cunning was demonstrated in the manner in which she did away with her young husband, probably to satisfy a personal enmity or to seek a fairer partner."[144]

Elizabeth Ziolkowski may not have been a model wife, but she was a model prisoner in the Detroit House of Correction. She was so well liked, her fellow prisoners once voted her "Woman of the Year." She learned how to write her name and put her seamstress skills to work by sewing

American flags, one of which ended up flying from the Detroit City Hall. She also made a black satin dress that she planned to wear to her upcoming parole hearing but eventually decided against wearing black. She squirreled away her pay—$0.25 per hour—and managed to amass $735 in cash and bonds.

A deeply pious Catholic, Ziolkowski never missed a Sunday service and decorated her cell with rosary beads and other tokens of her faith.

After serving twenty-eight years of her life sentence, Elizabeth Ziolkowski appeared to have a fighting chance with the parole board in 1961. "I haven't very long in this world," the eighty-five-year-old convicted murderer pled with the board, "and I'd like to be free."[145]

She maintained her innocence and claimed that her third husband's demise resulted from his use of arsenate of lead to treat his sores. He sometimes rubbed the poison into open wounds, a practice Elizabeth said other people—including his mother—witnessed. She added that at the time, she couldn't read or write and did not know the bottle contained poison.

She also addressed the untimely death of her second husband, John Boston, whose exhumation in 1932 led to the discovery of poison in his system. He died, she insisted, from a heart attack. "He always had heart trouble when he was drinking," she said.[146]

While news of John Ziolkowski's murder did not travel far from the western Upper Peninsula, his widow's push for freedom made headlines across the country. As the oldest woman incarcerated in Michigan, the elderly prisoner offered an enticing angle for journalists who prominently featured the number eighty-five when writing about her.

In April, Governor John B. Swainson signed a document commuting Elizabeth Ziolkowski's sentence to ninety years, which made her eligible for parole. She left prison later that spring and went to live with a daughter who operated a retirement home.

Elizabeth Ziolkowski's unwavering claim of innocence must be tempered by the multiple versions she presented. In the first rendition, she administered the poison at John's request because he believed it would ease his crippling stomach pains. In the second rendition, she mixed poison in John's drink to save her granddaughter from his advances and to punish him for bringing home a social disease. In the third, she said that John died of an accidental overdose when he applied arsenate of lead to open sores in an attempt to treat them.

Which version was correct? Elizabeth Ziolkowski took the answer to that question with her when she died in 1964 at the age of eighty-eight.

9
THREE SIRENS
DETROIT, 1935

The *Detroit Free Press* called it "the strangest crime ever to be committed in Detroit," and that is really saying something.[147]

The body was discovered before daybreak on Thursday, June 27, 1935. He had been dead for about ninety minutes.

The dead man lay face-down, sprawled out in the tall grass by the intersection of Joy Road and Picnic Drive—a remote windswept plain in the River Rouge Park. Clothed except for his suit jacket and overcoat, the victim appeared to be a middle-aged man of medium build and height. Two bullets from a .38 had sealed his lips: one in the left side of the chest and one in the head, execution-style.

Gunpowder residue—a dark ring of around the entry wound in the head—indicated that the killer stood or sat close to the victim. There was a thunderstorm earlier that morning, yet the clothes on the body were dry. This and the lack of any blood at the scene hinted that the victim had been shot in the back seat of a car and his body dumped.

The victim's wallet was missing, but because the perpetrator did not take a gold watch or two gold tokens inscribed "je porte bonheur" ("I bring good luck"), robbery did not appear a likely motive. The crime scene had all the hallmarks of an underworld hit.

The gold watch and high-quality shoes suggested the victim was affluent. The serial numbers on both articles would later help detectives establish the dead man's identity.

Two miles away from the scene, investigators found a tan overcoat. A hole in the breast corresponded with the gunshot wound on the victim's chest. Inside one of the pockets was a key to room 2422 at the swanky Book-Cadillac Hotel.

The swanky Book-Cadillac Hotel, where Howard Carter Dickinson would meet the sirens who would lead him to his doom. *Library of Congress.*

Room 2422 belonged to Howard Carter Dickinson, an affluent New York lawyer and the nephew to Charles Evans Hughes, the chief justice of the U.S. Supreme Court. Serial numbers on the shoes and gold watch proved that they belonged to Dickinson, and the manager of the Book-Cadillac dispelled any doubt when he identified the body. The dead man was Dickinson.

The fifty-two-year-old lawyer had made frequent business trips to Detroit during the previous months to investigate a bizarre claim on the Croesus-like fortune of William H. Yawkey. A lumber baron and one-time co-owner of the Detroit Tigers, Yawkey had a reputation as a playboy and frequented the hot nightspots of both Manhattan and Detroit. Around 1905, he began a long-standing relationship with a divorcée named Margaret Draper. The couple moved to New York and married in 1911. Unable to have a child, they adopted a little boy.

Yawkey passed away in 1919, leaving the bulk of his fortune to his widow and his adopted son, Thomas. The will also allotted $500,000 for any children that resulted from his union to Margaret.

After Margaret died in 1933, a woman came forward, claiming to be Yawkey's love child with Margaret before they moved to New York and married. According to the claim, Yawkey wanted to avoid the negative publicity of an illegitimate child and gave the baby girl to his friend James Carmichael, who raised the girl as his own. Elizabeth Carmichael Witherspoon, an actress, knew she had been adopted but didn't know about her true parentage until after Margaret Yawkey's death. She claimed that the names of the mother and father on her 1907 birth certificate were pseudonyms for William Yawkey and Margaret Draper, which entitled her to a portion of Yawkey's massive legacy.[148] Dickinson was in charge of defending the estate against the Witherspoon claim and, in the months leading up to his murder, made numerous trips to Detroit, where he conducted interviews and took depositions.

Dickinson was rumored to carry large sums of cash on his person. According to his wife, Marjorie, Dickinson traveled to Detroit with several thousand dollars in cash. Detectives, however, did not find even one greenback in his room.

The lawyer apparently liked to play the role of big shot attorney. His client—the $40 million William H. Yawkey estate—provided his street cred. A few rounds or a dinner or two for a friend or acquaintance, paid for with fives and tens flipped from a bankroll, solidified his reputation as a big spender who carried a wad of cash. Even though he didn't.

"Howard Carter Dickinson was a frail undersized man with a pronounced inferiority complex," according to an impromptu diagnosis by a *Free Press* reporter. "Scholarly, timid, he had experienced a bitter and hard life. Though related to wealth he had none of his own, and pride compelled him to carry on alone."[149]

Howard Carter Dickinson worked in a caviar and Delmonico world but ate his lunch out of a brown paper bag. He had champagne tastes and a beer budget but liked to present himself as an aristocrat. This made him a mark.

Working backward, detectives pieced together a timeline for Dickinson's movements since he arrived in Detroit the previous Tuesday. They managed to account for every hour until nine thirty on Wednesday evening, when he failed to show up for an appointment with fellow lawyers.

According to hotel employees, sometime around 9:30 p.m. on Wednesday, June 26, Dickinson left the hotel. It was the last time anyone saw him alive. Eight hours later, his bullet-riddled corpse was discovered on a lonely, remote road. Investigators had no idea what occurred during the missing eight hours in Dickinson's timeline.

They did have one provocative clue. At 4:00 p.m. on Thursday—ten hours after the discovery of Dickinson's body—an unidentified woman brought his suitcase to the check room of the Book-Cadillac. That particular time was rush hour at the check room, with people checking in and checking out of the hotel, so the clerk could remember nothing about the woman's appearance.

The woman could likely fill in some of the missing hours and lead investigators to the trigger finger, but investigators had no clue as to her identity. A *Free Press* reporter wryly commented on their dilemma: "She may be tall or short, willowy or squat, old or young, blond, brunet or titian. She may have the dress and manners of a mannequin. She may be dowdy."[150]

The break in the Dickinson case came when investigators located a cab driver named Andrew Smygen. Police tracked the cabbie through a phone call to a room at the Detroiter Hotel.

After Dickinson arrived in Detroit on Tuesday, he made two calls from his Book-Cadillac room, both to a room in the Detroiter Hotel. Detectives tapped the phone and listened in when Smygen called the occupant—a man he knew as Taylor—to inquire about a check. They traced the call to the Mayfair Theater, where they found the cab driver.

The cabbie recalled meeting a man whom he knew as "James Taylor" on Wednesday afternoon. As Smygen walked to the cab garage, Taylor stopped and offered him a lift. During the ride, Taylor commented that he and two female acquaintances had planned a party for "a lawyer named Dickinson from the Book-Cadillac." He also said that the lawyer had a lot of money.[151] Smygen could make a few bucks, Taylor suggested, by chauffeuring the entourage around town.

"I thought about his wife," Smygen told investigators, "but I didn't think I'd say anything because I figured the guy was picking up some money on the side by providing entertainment. It wasn't any of my business, anyhow."

Although Taylor didn't name his "female acquaintances," he hinted at their specific role in the party at the Detroiter when he described them as "high class. They don't foot with no small money guys."[152] The still unidentified women apparently acted as a honey trap in a robbery scheme.

Following Taylor's suggestion about a possible fare, Smygen drove his taxi to the Detroiter. At about 9:00 p.m., Taylor emerged from the hotel, telling the cabbie that his two female friends were "entertaining a big-shot lawyer who lived at the Book-Cadillac" and they would not need his services. Taylor tipped him fifty cents, and the unsuspecting cab driver left.

The mysterious man did not strike Smygen as a killer. "As I remember him I didn't think he looked like the sort of guy who'd kill anybody. His clothes didn't bulge like he carried a gun and he didn't talk tough or anything."[153]

"James Taylor" was one of the many aliases of William Schweitzer, a con man with an arm-long rap sheet.

Schweitzer's estranged wife Violet was nine months' pregnant and lived in an apartment on Fourth and Kirby Avenues, but she told police that her husband hadn't lived there for the past three weeks. He spent that period living out of a room in the Detroiter, where he often spent time with two lady friends that hotel personnel described as lithe beauties with reddish hair.

Schweitzer checked out of the Detroiter at the crack of dawn on Thursday—at about the same time that Dickinson's body was discovered at River Rouge Park—and according to a hotel bellhop, he appeared in a highly agitated state.[154]

Twenty-six-year-old William Schweitzer, who also went by a half-dozen aliases, including William Lee Ferris, was a handsome man who drew parallels to John Dillinger. A wanted notice by the Detroit Police described the suspect as "age 26 (looks 33), height 5 feet 6 or 7 inches, weight 145 pounds, medium complexion, dark brown hair, blue eyes, good teeth, armed and dangerous."[155]

Schweitzer had several priors and a police file half an inch thick. His lengthy rap sheet included car theft, check fraud and a murder he committed five years earlier when he shot a man who attempted to rob him. He beat the rap by claiming self-defense. In June 1935, he was in dire need of quick cash.

After checking out of the Detroiter, Schweitzer was believed to have left Detroit in the company of two redheaded women that police identified as Florence and Loretta Jackson, but detectives had no idea of their whereabouts until one of the redheads—Loretta Jackson—sent a telegram from Fort Wayne to her mother in Detroit. "Having a swell vacation," she noted. "Everything fine. Be home in a week."[156]

Detectives followed the trail to the Rich Hotel and four shadowy guests registered under pseudonyms the "Mayer Sisters" of Grand Rapids, Michigan, and "Art Reynald" of Kansas City.

Detectives collared the four characters in Fort Wayne on Saturday, June 29. To the media legion that showed up to greet the car transporting the suspects, Schweitzer appeared a man without a worry in the world; he walked with a swagger, told jokes and hammed it up with reporters. Off camera, he was a bundle of nerves, sulky, morose and unwilling to discuss Dickinson. It was all a matter of mistaken identity, he said, and insisted that he wasn't in Detroit on the night in question.

Twenty-seven-year-old Loretta "Bobbie" Jackson was an auburn-haired beauty, a former burlesque dancer and allegedly Schweitzer's sweetheart. (She later denied it.) She began dancing at age five to help the family make ends meet, which was difficult after her father drank up his paycheck at the nearest corner tavern. A three-time divorcée, she married her first husband at age fifteen, her second at age nineteen and had two children from her third but left them in the custody of her elderly mother most of the time. According to Anna Jackson's apartment superintendent, Loretta did not live in the apartment but dropped by once or twice a week to change her clothes.[157] Police eyed the mother of two as one of Dickinson's entertainers at the party in Schweitzer's hotel room.

The elder Jackson sister claimed to be engaged to a Ford employee, although she wanted to keep his name out of the press. "I don't want to tell you his name," she whined to a *Detroit Times* reporter. "I don't want to tell you his name. I don't want to drag him into it. He works at Ford's and he is still standing by me. In spite of all this, he worships the ground I walk on."[158]

Bobbie Jackson had none of her unnamed boyfriend's swagger. The arrest left her teetering on the edge of a nervous breakdown. It was reported that she fainted three times while en route to Detroit.

The other entertainer was Loretta's twenty-four-year-old kid sister Florence or "Flossie." Like Bobbie, hard times brought an early end to her childhood. Forced to leave school in the eighth grade, she began dancing at the age of fourteen. She was married although estranged from her husband, their relationship a casualty of unemployment and the Great Depression.

Although three years apart in age, the two Jackson sisters could pass for twins. They both had auburn-tinted hair that they wore shoulder-length and parted on the left side, although Flossie tucked her hair behind her ears. When the case made headlines, newspapermen weren't particularly kind about the Jackson sisters. One reporter described them as "not pretty," "not even well dressed" and "thin, flat chested, scrawny."[159] Both women claimed to be heavy drinkers, and both blamed the genie in the bottle for stealing their souls on that fateful night when Dickinson attended his last party.

The Jackson sisters lived in a dingy third-floor flat on Parsons Street with their ailing sixty-five-year-old mother, who watched after Bobbie's two children. The aged woman, suffering from a bout of pneumonia, refused to believe her daughters guilty of any wrongdoing. "They've always been good girls," she told a *Times* reporter. "Why should they get mixed up in a mess like this?" The naïve Jackson matriarch denied that the "good girls" worked burlesque. "The girls are tap dancers. They get occasional engagements in beer gardens and cafes."[160]

The third in the trio of women was twenty-one-year-old Jean Miller, a former school chum of Flossie Jackson, whom she had known ever since they met as gangly youths in the fourth grade. Miller regarded Bobbie Jackson as an older sister. "I remember when I got a job first in show business," she later recalled, "she taught me tap dancing and she made the rest of the girls stop teasing me."[161]

She was married but like Flossie Jackson separated from her husband. And like Flossie Jackson, she cited dire financial straits as the cause of her breakup and heavy drinking as her undoing.[162] Her exact role in the Dickinson case remained a mystery. All the police really knew about her was that like Schweitzer, she had several aliases.

All three women dreamed of a life under the limelights and apparently came to believe that Bill Schweitzer could provide the break they needed. He apparently suggested a touring tent show revue. The only thing missing was the startup money. Schweitzer knew exactly where he could get it, but he would need the girls.

Following the principle of divide and conquer, Detroit detectives separated Schweitzer from the three women and began interrogations. To solve the

When the Dickinson murder became front-page news in 1935, the Jackson sisters became subjects of fascination among the public, including one news photographer who captured a sullen, dejected Flossie Jackson…

case, they needed to understand why a prestigious New York lawyer—a father, husband and legal champion of a $40 million estate—would consort with a career criminal and three women of dubious reputation. It seemed highly unlikely that the upright Dickinson would go to the Detroiter to socialize with Schweitzer alone. On the other hand, Schweitzer's sirens—three attractive and leggy nymphets—may have provided a lure simply too strong for the middle-aged married man to resist.

The tight-lipped con man at first refused to acknowledge even knowing Dickinson, but investigators had more luck with the women. Bobbie Jackson said that she and her sister first met Dickinson in the dining room of the Book-Cadillac when he offered to buy them a round. When Schweitzer, who was with the Jackson sisters at the time, left, the two women went up to Dickinson's room. A few hours later, they went to a nearby café, where they once again met Schweitzer, who drove Dickinson back to the Book-Cadillac after arranging a party at the Detroiter the following night.

Jean Miller claimed to have joined the party just before they left the Detroiter. Unhinged by the interrogations, she had a nervous fit that caused police to take her to a hospital, where a bracer of opiates restored her nerves.

The women told of an alcohol-fueled game of strip poker in Schweitzer's room on Wednesday night, which Dickinson lost. At the end of the game, he was left wearing nothing but his socks, his shoes and his modesty. What actually transpired behind closed doors of Schweitzer's hotel room remains lost to history, but it is likely that the revelries went beyond a card game. "He was pretty fresh with us girls," Bobbie Jackson later recalled.[163]

Dirty details aside, a clearer picture of Dickinson's demise began to materialize from the mass of conflicting stories told by the four suspects. At some point in the evening, around nine o'clock, Schweitzer went to the hotel lobby, leaving Dickinson alone with the three women (so they could become "better acquainted," he later said) and dismissed Smygen, who arrived on cue at the Detroiter expecting a large fare.

Dickinson, flanked by Flossie Jackson and Jean Miller, crawled into the back seat of Schweitzer's car and headed to a nearby watering hole for a nightcap. Schweitzer

...and her forlorn sister Loretta, who avoided making eye contact with the camera. *Library of Congress.*

drove with Bobbie Jackson perched in the front passenger's seat. Once inside the River Rouge Park, Schweitzer pulled over and commanded the women to get out. "What's this all about?" Dickinson exclaimed while Schweitzer shimmied into the back seat next to him. Pulling a .38 from his jacket pocket, Schweitzer jammed the barrel into the mystified lawyer's ribs and pulled the trigger. Dickinson slumped across the seat, and Schweitzer put an insurance round in the dead lawyer's forehead. He slid Dickinson's wallet out of his pocket and deposited the body on the side of the road.

The three women told stories that varied only in the minutest of details. They all agreed on one point: none of them knew that Schweitzer planned to take Dickinson for his final ride. After the shooting, they wanted to leave, but Schweitzer threatened them. He managed to cow them into complicity after the fact by scaring them into thinking they were "in it" with him.

Confronted by the stories told by the women, Schweitzer fessed up to spending the evening partying with Dickinson, although he maintained that the shooting was an accident. The .38 belonged to the lawyer, who pulled it from his pocket when the women (in Schweitzer's rendition) asked to exit the vehicle. Somehow the gun discharged, killing Dickinson instantly.

"I reached in and pulled him by the arm," Schweitzer said. "When I pulled him part way out, his coat came off. Then the gun went off a second time as I was dragging him to the ground." The bogus story, however, did not present a reasonable explanation for the location of the bullet entry wounds. Besides, Dickinson did not own a firearm.

"The reason why I ran away," Schweitzer explained, "is because of my bad reputation and I knew they'd try to pin something on me."

Schweitzer had a spin for everything, even for the significant differences in the various stories he had told. "The reason I told the other stories to the detectives is this: I didn't think it mattered what I told them anyway, because the Prosecutor wasn't there so it wouldn't be legal."[164]

Once convinced that a bigger game than mere robbery lay behind Dickinson's gangland-style slaying, detectives now believed that the lawyer's death resulted from the rumor that he carried large sums of cash. A career criminal, short of money, enlisted the help of three beauties to lure Dickinson into a party that ended with two bullets in the River Rouge Park. Since Dickinson did not in fact carry a large sum, his murderer netted only a paltry one hundred dollars and change.

Two questions remained. Schweitzer pulled the trigger, but what led the blue-blooded family man to rub elbows with the earthier characters from the seedier side of Detroit? And Schweitzer evidently needed the women to entice Dickinson, but did they know what he had planned?

According to a seasoned beat writer for the *Detroit Times*, the Jackson sisters were slow on the uptake and putty in the hands of the manipulative Schweitzer. Had they contacted the police after the shooting, they would have been nothing more than material witnesses. But they didn't go to the authorities—they ran.

By Monday, July 1, time behind bars had taken its toll on the three women. Bobbie and Flossie Jackson appeared haggard and tired, but Jean Miller teetered on the edge of a breakdown.

One by one, they broke under the relentless questioning.[165] Jean Miller broke first, but it was Flossie Jackson's statement that was the most specific

Schweitzer's three sirens in the limelight at last: Loretta Jackson, Jean Miller, and Florence Jackson. *Author's collection.*

and the most damning. "I did not tell the truth in my first statement," Flossie Jackson admitted. "I was trying to hide it. I want to the tell the truth now."

The new truth according to the younger Jackson sister included several admissions. She and Bobbie first suggested the plan to "roll" Dickinson or "knock him out," but Schweitzer objected. Dickinson would later identify them, so Schweitzer insisted that the only safe thing was to kill him.

"There was some argument about that," she said, "but we finally decided to let Bill get his gun and we'd take him out. We decided to kill him."

Jean Miller, Flossie said, wanted to go along with the plan, but they neglected to tell her that they planned to kill Dickinson. Miller went into the night believing that it would end with a strong-arm robbery of an intoxicated victim. The only one hurt would be Dickinson's pocketbook. They agreed on a prearranged signal. Jean Miller would ask Schweitzer to stop the car so she could get some air, and the robbery would commence.

Flossie also wiped away any possibility of an accidental shooting by describing Schweitzer administering a coup de grace: "Dickinson fell to

Detectives examine the murder scene: the car in which Howard Carter Dickinson was murdered. *Author's collection*.

the ground then, and Bill fired a shot into his head while he was standing over him."

The women rifled through the dead man's pockets and found just $120. Disappointed, Schweitzer commented, "That's a hell of a small amount to kill a man for. I thought they'd be some fifties in there. But he won't talk any more."[166]

Two days in a cell and forty hours of nearly nonstop questioning had turned the debonair wannabe Dillinger into a sniveling, cowering shadow of his former self. The mental strain had a pronounced effect on Schweitzer's physical appearance. His chin drooped, his smile faded as the corners of his lips dropped, and his eyes widened. He was scared.

Schweitzer dropped all pretense and confessed to playing a con on the supposedly rich lawyer. On Tuesday, he and the Jackson sisters, he said, talked about Dickinson:

> We thought he was a rich man, because he was a lawyer from New York and was staying at the Book. He talked kind of big and made us think he was pretty important.
>
> We began to think that we could get a lot of money from him if we robbed him. We talked about it all that evening in my hotel room, and were up pretty late.
>
> It was sometime in the early hours of Wednesday morning when I arranged this job with Florence and Loretta. I proposed the holdup.
>
> I said to them: "Why don't we get him, take him out and roll him? I've got a gun." One of the sisters spoke up, I don't know which one, and said: "Can't we knock him over the head instead?" I said, "No, that's too dangerous."
>
> So we decided we'd use the gun and at a signal one of the girls would stay in the car with Dickinson and myself. I don't remember which girl was to stay in the car, but I think it was Florence.
>
> When two of the girls got out of the car I put the gun on Dickinson without saying anything. Dickinson seemed stunned and the gun went off, and it went off a second time as I was pulling off Dickinson's coat and vest. I fired a third shot at his head when he was on the ground beside the car.[167]

As for role the women played, a *Free Press* reporter envisioned the "hook" in the swanky dining room of the Book-Cadillac:

Howard Carter Dickinson ordered straight whisky. He swallowed quickly and choked a bit. One of the girls turned directly toward him and she laughed merrily at his discomfiture. He smiled back. She smiled her sweetest. The racket was on.

Howard Carter Dickinson was a lonely little man in a strange city. He craved company. Why not? There was an extra girl at the table. That is the way the game is worked. They all smiled at him now. The drinks he had had made the whole world look rosy—made these two poor drab girls look lovely. Courteously he asked the privilege of buying them a drink—the little joke was on him.[168]

Dickinson's rose-tinted whiskey glasses would cost him his life.

Reporters tended to view the women with ambivalence. They helped bring off a cold-blooded murder, but they were dupes to Schweitzer's masterful manipulation.

"No two women ever looked less like murderers than these two blousy little hat racks," wrote a *Free Press* reporter. "But they were dominated by Schweitzer, the bad man, the boy who boasted of his crimes and his meanness. They feared him and they obeyed him." Schweitzer knew that the women dreamed of a life in showbiz and preyed on that dream by promising them the break they needed.[169]

Prosecutor Duncan C. McCrea decided to charge all four defendants with first-degree murder, which meant a mandatory life sentence. All four pleaded not guilty, ensuring a trial rather than the quick denouement McCrea envisioned. To avoid spending the remainder of their lives in prison, they would need to find some way to counteract their admissions. Almost in unison, they screamed "coercion." The women claimed that their confessions resulted from extreme sleep deprivation, which made them vulnerable to suggestion.

"We didn't sleep for four days and four nights," Bobbie Jackson complained. "We didn't even have our clothes off. None of us knew what we were saying. They kept promising us they'd let us alone if we'd tell them what they wanted."[170]

Schweitzer went a step further when he claimed that detectives beat him into confessing. They manhandled him and withheld food, essentially starving him into submission. They buried their fists in his stomach and smashed his head against the wall.

The con man's testimony came in three parts: besmirching the victim's reputation, presenting an alternate scenario to the shooting and tarring the police for browbeating him into confessing to a crime he didn't commit.

To hear Schweitzer tell it, Dickinson was a wannabe playboy with a large appetite for booze and broads. He related an incident in Dickinson's room when they didn't have enough cups, so the attorney offered to drink whiskey from Bobbie Jackson's shoe. But Bobbie was no Cinderella and Dickinson no Prince Charming. Rather, he was an ogre who later insisted on a game of strip poker.

"After coaxing," Schweitzer testified, "the women agreed to play. We used the bed as a card table. We told stories and joked as we played, and had some drinks. We agreed that when one person lost all his clothes we would stop playing."[171]

To counter the claims of police brutality, McCrea planned to read the confessions into the record. Before allowing McCrea to proceed, Judge John A. Boyne turned the proceeding into an NC-17 affair by banning anyone under the age of sixteen. After Boyne's proclamation, a handful of disappointed youth shuffled out of the courtroom.

All three women took the stand and described enduring third-degree-style tactics. The Jackson sisters performed well, but Jean Miller's turn on the stand unbalanced her. She collapsed during McCrea's cross-examination, particularly at the moment when he accused her of acting. After a thirty-minute recess and treatment by a doctor, she returned to the stand.

Even the loudest and most dramatic histrionics could not drown out the sound of the four conspirators confessing, as channeled through the medium of Duncan McCrea.

After three weeks of listening to testimony, the jury went into deliberations in mid-August and returned after five hours. Jean Miller, true to form, collapsed upon hearing the jury foreman proclaim her guilty. The Jackson sisters made several banshee-like shrieks and then audibly sobbed, and the four hundred spectators that packed into the Recorder's Courtroom erupted in applause. The cacophony drowned out the foreman's recommendation of leniency for the three women. The jurors—six men and six women—evidently saw Schweitzer as the prime mover in the robbery-homicide plot.

Schweitzer, stunned by the decision, remained expressionless, his lips gelled into a half-smile, half-frown.

The sentencing was anticlimactic, since the verdict triggered mandatory life sentences. Schweitzer made the lengthy journey north to the state penitentiary at Marquette, while the women traveled only a few miles to the Detroit House of Correction in Northville.

After the trial concluded, the court psychiatrist's report on the four now convicted slayers became public. In his report, Dr. I.L. Polozker characterized Schweitzer as an egomaniac with a mental age of twelve and an IQ of 78. He considered Schweitzer highly dangerous and recommended the parole board never free him.

Polozker described the women as "infantile, unstable and unsocial." Loretta Jackson was the most intelligent of the three, followed by Jean Miller, who suffered from "psychoneurosis" and "hysteria." Florence Jackson had the lowest mental age of the three.[172]

It wasn't exactly the hardest time for Bobbie and Flossie Jackson, who ended up living in a matron's suite with a private bath. These comparatively luxurious accommodations, for which prison matrons paid but the convicted murderesses (along with a fellow slayer Hildegarde Sundell, who earned her life sentence after a robbery led to the death of a policeman) received courtesy of the state, raised eyebrows and led to an official probe in 1948.

The prison superintendent waved away the criticism by explaining that the Jackson sisters ran the dining hall and that these duties caused them to rise earlier than the other inmates.[173] Jean Miller's work in the beauty shop did not garner such special treatment.

Serious discussion of freedom for the three women first began in 1950, after they had spent the better part of fifteen years in prison. In December, the parole board gave them an early Christmas present. Forty-four-year-old Bobbie, thirty-nine-year-old Flossie and thirty-six-year-old Jean Miller left the House. They planned to put their time to good use. The Jackson sisters wanted to open a tearoom, and Jean Miller planned to open a salon.

In 1965, William Schweitzer made a bid for freedom after spending thirty years in prison. He was fifty-seven, his hairline had receded and he relied on a pair of horn-rimmed glasses to see. He had spent a good part of his time teaching school to fellow convicts and looked the part.

A judge allowed him to appeal his verdict on a recent change in the law that required trial judges and not juries to determine the legality and admissibility of confessions obtained by law enforcement. Schweitzer also claimed that sensationalized news items made it impossible to empanel an unprejudiced jury.

After an exhaustive search, no one could find the official trial transcript. The transcript for one of the premier headline trials of Depression-era

Detroit was missing, possibly plucked from the haphazard cardboard box filing system at the court building and freely available to anyone who cared to take the elevator or walk the steps to the sixth floor. So, the beleaguered convict had to rely on the same sensationalized newspaper accounts he criticized as tainting his jury in the first place. Ultimately, Schweitzer prevailed and regained his freedom. He died a free man on May 26, 1997, at the age of seventy-four.

Bobbie and Flossie Jackson and their school chum Jean Miller dreamed of a star billing as the "Jackson Sisters." For three weeks in 1935, they had center stage in Detroit, but the *Recorder*'s courtroom wasn't quite the venue they had envisioned.

Writing about the case in 1945, longtime *Free Press* police reporter Patrick S. McDougall expressed sympathy for the trio, casting them as victims rather than perpetrators.

"Dull, dispirited, morally blunted," McDougall wrote, "they could be persuaded into anything by anyone stronger than they."[174]

Enter Bill Schweitzer, who suffered from a two-bit Napoleon complex. After intoxicating the impressionable showgirls with visions of stardust, he reveled in the power he could exert over the three women. He viewed them as nothing but tools to be discarded later if it suited his purpose.

McDougall notes that without Schweitzer, the women would have led a crime-free life. The overpowering force of Schweitzer's gravity pulled them into black hole that led to a downward spiral ending with the dead man face down in a meadow.

Statements from the four principal players in the Dickinson tragedy leave very little doubt that the women knew what would happen when they climbed into Schweitzer's car. They knew it was wrong, yet they played along anyway.

In fact, it is improbable that Schweitzer could have duped the libidinous lawyer without the three attractive waifs at this side.

10

YOU BELONG TO ME

MURDER OF THE LOVE SLAVE
ANN ARBOR, 1936

Betty Baker described the love triangle with an elementary school ABC: "A is for Al, B is for Betty and C is for Cub."[175] It wasn't child's play she had in mind, however, when she drove her lover "Cub" to a lonely road in Scio Township on June 29, 1936.

Betty Baker, also known as "Bum Bum," was born Myrtle A. Douglas in 1906. Considered a beauty when she became fodder for front page news stories in 1937, the one-time Miss Ann Arbor was described by reporters as "willowy," "lithe" and "sultry." Her large eyes, pencil-thin eyebrows, high cheekbones and oval-shaped face made her a dead ringer for a young Bette Davis.

The Bette Davis lookalike worked as a dancer in Detroit during the Roaring Twenties. She married Albert K. Baker, a cab driver from Ann Arbor, in 1929. Their marriage was still in the honeymoon phase when she met Clarence Schneider.

Betty worked as a supervisor of student employees at the Helen Newberry residence hall. Schneider, Betty said, was smitten with her and wouldn't take "no" for an answer. She tried to discourage his advances and even arranged dates with other women, but Schneider believed he had found his soulmate. "I'll love you all my life," he once told her.[176]

Betty couldn't resist. They began to see each other behind Albert's back. They did an excellent job hiding the affair, which by the summer of 1936, had lasted six years—almost the entire span of Betty's marriage to Albert.

In 1935, Schneider moved into the attic of the Baker residence as a boarder, which brought the lovers even closer together. The cuckolded husband, who had traded his cabbie's license for a badge when he became an Ann Arbor police officer, did not know or even suspect that his wife was fooling around with his best friend. Sometimes, Betty would arrange dates for "Cub" Schneider, and the two couples would paint the town red.

Albert remained blissfully ignorant of his wife's infidelity. "I thought it was a happy marriage so far as I knew," he later recalled. "She once asked me if I wanted a divorce. That was because she was so nervous. She has been that way for three or four years."[177]

As the affair progressed, Betty's affection for Schneider became an obsession. She loved Albert, she would later explain, but came to view Schneider as her soulmate. Betty planned to divorce Albert and marry Cub, but she just couldn't bring herself to break Albert's heart. Besides, she didn't trust Cub, who, she was convinced, saw other women behind her back.

When Betty heard rumors about Schneider seeing other women, she began stalking him. She visited his place of work and interrogated Cub's coworkers about his love life. She compiled a short list of Schneider's possible girlfriends along with dates he most likely saw them. Once when Clarence's brother borrowed his car for a period of forty-six minutes, Betty checked the speedometer and noted that it had traveled forty-seven miles. She accused Cub of parking with another woman. On more than one occasion, she brandished her husband's service revolver, waving the weapon to scare her lover. Once, Clarence yanked the revolver from Betty's grip and slapped her.

At four thirty on the afternoon of June 29, Betty confronted Clarence at the restaurant where he worked. Noticing his newly shined shoes and neatly combed hair, she accused him of running around on her. Following a brief but heated expletive-filled exchange during which Clarence called his lover a "damned nag," Betty stormed out, climbed into her car and drove home. Careful not to rouse Albert from a deep slumber, she wrapped his revolver in a newspaper and drove back to the restaurant.

Betty coaxed Clarence into the car and drove him to a secluded spot on Wagner Road near Huron River Drive.

About thirty minutes later, Betty pulled her car into the garage at their residence with a dead man in the back seat. This time, she woke Albert and told him "something terrible had happened," although she did not tell him that his best friend's body was in the garage. Betty said they needed to call "Shanny"—Milton G. Schancupp, a friend of the family and assistant attorney general for the State of Michigan—and ask him to make the trip from Lansing.

When Schancupp arrived, Albert telephoned the police.

Around 9:30 p.m., Washtenaw County coroner E.C. Ganzhorn arrived at the Baker residence to examine the body. A single bullet had entered Schneider's skull below his nose, tore a path through his brain and became lodged in the back seat. He died instantly.

While Ganzhorn examined Schneider's body, prosecutor Albert Rapp interviewed Betty Baker. She admitted taking her husband's gun to scare Schneider. She pulled back the hammer and was shaking the gun at Schneider when it accidentally discharged. She planned to take him to the hospital, but when she realized that the shot was fatal, she went home instead.

Something about Betty Baker's story was fishy, so she was brought to the county jail for further questioning.

Baker stayed true to her accidental shooting story, but investigators uncovered enough evidence to convince Rapp to charge her with first-degree murder.

Weapons experts claimed that Baker's service revolver contained a safety device that made it impossible to fire without pulling the trigger, a powerful piece of physical evidence that undermined Betty Baker's accidental shooting.

The trial took place in January 1937. The seedy melodrama had all the necessary elements of a dime novel: the attractive but possessive dancer, her young and handsome paramour, the cuckolded cop and an illicit affair that ended with a single gunshot. Betty Baker became an overnight sensation.

Spectators descended on the courthouse to watch the best theater in town, but aware of possibly ribald testimony, Judge George W. Sample excluded anyone under the age of twenty-one.

Rapp laid out his theory for the jury:

> I'll prove that when Schneider was between 16 and 17, and she was a married woman, she got him under her control. I'll prove that for six years they were sweethearts.
>
> I will show she even went to a certain Ann Arbor physician and wanted to know where was the best place to kill a man.
>
> Betty Baker made up her mind no one else was going to have Clarence Schneider, if she couldn't have him. Why, she even induced him to move to

her home a year ago. There wasn't room for him and he had to sleep on a davenport, but she wanted him there close to her.[178]

The prosecutor characterized Betty Baker as a "Circe"—an evil sorceress capable of transforming men into wild animals—and Cub as her "love slave."

Rapp proceeded to call witnesses whom he believed would leave no lingering doubt that Betty Baker planned the murder ahead of time. Some of the most damaging testimony to Baker's defense came from Dr. Joseph H. Failing, who repeated an ominous conversation with the defendant.

"She came up one day about two years ago to my office," Dr. Failing explained, "and said that she was angry at someone and that he should be shot.

"I said, 'Well, if you're going to shoot any one, shoot him between the eyes. That is sure death.' It was said jokingly," added the physician, "and assumed no significance until she did shoot someone."[179]

Betty kept her composure as she listened to the prosecution witnesses paint a picture of an obsessive, possessive siren who would do anything, including murder, to keep her boy toy from other women. At times, she even appeared lighthearted. When Judge Sample adjourned court on Wednesday, she strode to the witness stand and dropped into the chair. "Maybe they'll let me take it home to practice sitting in," she quipped.[180]

The pivotal moment in the trial came when Betty Baker took the stand for real. Albert sat in the front row of the gallery and listened to his wife profess her love and affection for his best friend. He would later claim that he first learned of the affair during Betty's testimony.

"When I first met him," Betty testified, "'Cub' was a gawky, ungainly boy—five years younger than I. I polished him up and taught him manners. I used to enjoy having him put me on a pedestal."[181]

Betty explained that her relationship with Cub wasn't just a fling or a tryst; it was true love. "Our love affair was never cheap. It was beautiful because it was sincere. Both 'Cub' and I were of the temperament which can not tolerate intimacy without love."[182]

Betty characterized Cub as the aggressor in the relationship. "I told him he was just a child, that I was his first love," she explained. "I said, 'Are you aware of the fact that I have a husband?' He said, 'Are you aware of the fact that I love you?' He would waylay me and talk to me about love."

"We were often together at my home and other places," Betty explained. "Our intimacy continued for five years. My husband never knew it."

Reporters did not note Albert Baker's expression during this portion of his wife's testimony, but he most likely cringed.

Betty described herself as trapped between her love for Cub and her affection for her husband, whom she began to view as more of a friend than a lover. From the witness stand, in a loud and clear voice, she declared her love for the dead man. "I was always fond of him (Schneider), though," she said. "I loved him and I loved my husband. Mr. Schneider's temperament suited me better than my husband's did."

Using expressions ripped from the pages of dime novels, Betty described her desperate attempts to ferret the truth from Cub with her husband's gun. "Once I took the gun and I said 'Cub, you are like the winds of the seven seas. You are not constant.' I frightened him and he told me the truth."

Betty described a second time when she pulled her husband's gun on Cub. He grabbed the gun out of her hands and pointed it at her. "I almost died. I dared him to pull the trigger. He said then he couldn't do that because he loved me. I told him the gun was unloaded. He looked to make sure and then we both had a good laugh."[183]

The third time, she testified, led to a tragic accident. Following the quarrel at the restaurant where Cub worked, she went home to fetch her husband's gun. "I tried to find someone to unload it, but couldn't," she explained. "When we got out on the River Road in the car I unwrapped it. He had laughed at me before because I didn't know how to handle a gun, so I pulled back the hammer just to show him."

"Then I talked to him, waving the gun up and down, just for emphasis. There was an explosion. I don't know whether my hand was on the trigger. I thought at first the explosion was outside. Then I saw he had fallen over. I thought he was trying to teach me a lesson."

During the cross-examination, Rapp handed Betty the smoking gun and asked her to demonstrate how the shooting occurred. "You say you don't know whether you touched the trigger. Try to make that gun go off without touching the trigger," Rapp said.[184]

Betty re-created the scene. She pulled back the hammer and hit it against the chair. Then she leveled the barrel and shook it vigorously. The hammer did not move.

Albert Baker followed his wife to the stand.

He described taking Betty to the shooting range and teaching her how to shoot his revolver. "I showed her once on the police range how to pull back the hammer and fire," he said. "She only shot it once."

Albert believed the shooting was accidental, but he did no favors for the defense when he explained that the trigger was easier to pull after he had the weapon oiled in April.

Betty's lawyer, John W. Conlin, arranged a graphic way to display the ease of pulling the trigger and therefore underline the possibility of an accidental discharge. He handed the weapon to juror no. 1 and asked him to pull the trigger. Then he passed the revolver to juror no. 2. All fourteen men in the jury box—twelve jurors and two alternates—tested the gun.

Betty's harshest critic during the trial was the man on the bench. Judge Sample offered a sharp, caustic editorial during a portion of his instructions to the jury.

Sample characterized Betty's affair with Cub as "an inordinate, morbid, illegal relationship which existed under the very eyes of the husband." He added, "Society couldn't live if it condoned such things. The jury should have no sympathy for such a so-called love dream. It doesn't deserve the classification."[185]

While anxiously awaiting her judgement, Betty took one final postmortem stab at Cub when she spoke with reporters.

"Al's done everything he could for me," she said. "He's a real man. Cub wasn't half the man Al is. Cub was sneaky. Why is it we fall in love with the heels?[186]

After seven ballots, the jury finally reached a consensus. All agreed on Betty's guilt, but they struggled to define her crime as first- or second-degree murder. A first-degree conviction came with a mandatory life sentence, whereas a second-degree murder verdict came with a possible life sentence at the discretion of the judge. Ultimately, the jury settled on second-degree murder. Judge Sample had to decide whether Betty received life or a lesser sentence.

Sample sentenced Betty to life.

Cornered by a reporter before deputies carted her away to jail, she said, "I don't exactly know how I feel. It was a rotten break."[187]

"I gave her the maximum," Judge Sample explained, "because I believed her a premeditated murderer of the worst type."[188]

When Betty Baker arrived at the Detroit House of Correction, she was greeted by a retinue of reporters. "I thought I was dead and buried as far as you're concerned," she remarked. "Well, I'm buried, all right."

She spoke about her husband, who met her at the Washtenaw County Jail to see her off to her new home in Northville. "Al has suffered terribly. He still loves me. He told me so. And I love him. I know that now. I wasn't myself. He is simply swellish."

"I haven't asked him to wait," Betty added. "That wouldn't be fair."

Still, she held out hope that her husband would still be her husband if she ever regained her freedom. "If they take my wedding ring away," she said, "it will be the first time I will have had it off since Al put it on my finger eight years ago. I feel it will be all over between us if they do." House of Correction regulations forbid the wearing of rings, so Betty had no choice but to remove her wedding band.

Nevertheless, Betty vowed to make the most of her new life. "I'm keeping my chin up. There is a lot you can learn in prison. You can see how the other half lives here. I mean it. It will be interesting, meeting all these girls who have done things, and analyzing them. I intend to be a good prisoner."[189]

When the "good prisoner" escaped by climbing over the prison fence in September 1939, rumors swirled that she intended to take revenge on Judge George Sample and prosecutor Albert Rapp, although she later laughed at the idea and said she planned to seek the legal advice of a criminal lawyer in New York.

She hid in the woods for two days before traveling east toward Detroit. After five days on the lam, she was captured at the intersection of Cass and Charlotte and returned to the prison. Her escape cost her thirty days in solitary confinement. After the escape, Betty settled down and served her time without incident.

In 1941, Betty's premonition about her wedding ring came true when Albert divorced her. He subsequently remarried and fathered two children.

"Bum Bum" Baker never wavered in her claim that Schneider's death was an accident. In 1956, she rehashed the story to a parole board, which decided to release her because she had a spotless record and a positive attitude. She left the House of Correction after serving nineteen years of her life sentence.

Betty's actions immediately after the shooting raise doubts about her sanity. She did not give Cub a pair of cement shoes and dump him in the Huron River. She did not dismember his body and stash the pieces. She made no attempt to cover up the murder at all, choosing instead to drive home with his corpse in the back seat as if she just could not part with it.

Betty Baker finally had her Cub just where she wanted.

11
HOUSDEN, WE HAVE A PROBLEM

DETROIT, 1944

I loved him so much that it was hell with him and hell without him," Nina Housden said about her marriage to Charles Housden.[190] She chose "hell without him" and plotted his exit for the evening of Monday, December 18, 1944.

Nina Housden crept up behind Charles as he was sitting in a kitchen chair. He outweighed her by sixty pounds, but she eliminated this advantage by serving him blackberry brandy spiked with a powerful soporific. By midnight, he had consumed over a fifth of the concoction. In a deep stupor, he did not notice his wife creeping up behind him with a coil of clothesline in her grip.

In one quick movement, Nina looped the clothesline over Charles's head, yanked it back toward her and twisted. Charles clawed at the rope, but Nina braced herself with one foot against the back of the chair and pulled as hard as she could. Her knuckles turned white, and the thin clothesline bit into her hands, but she ignored the pain. When she felt her grip slipping, she jabbed a knife into the knot and twisted it like a tourniquet.

Charles's face turned cyanotic and his body trembled. Then his arms dropped to his sides. He was dead.

Nina dragged Charles's body onto the bed and went for a walk. When she returned, she sat at the kitchen table, worked on a crossword puzzle and fell asleep.

Their happily-never-after began in Missouri, where Nina worked as a waitress in a local diner and Charles was stationed at a nearby military base.

She was born Nina Debaard in 1914, the oldest daughter of Kentucky farmer Jesse Debaard, whose plot of land was close to a neighboring farm owned by George Perkins. Perkins worked the land with help from his two sons: Jethro and Ventus. Nina and Ventus grew up together and may have been childhood sweethearts. In 1933, nineteen-year-old Nina married the twenty-one-year-old farm boy.[191]

Charles Rudolph Housden was born on November 8, 1915, in Calloway County, Kentucky. An excellent athlete, Charles played three years of basketball for New Concord High School before graduating with the class of 1934.

In April 1940, Charles married Modell Furgurson. Two years later, he was drafted into service. He saw combat in the Pacific theater before being billeted at a Missouri army base, where he met the brunette knockout destined to become his second wife.

It is unclear if and to what extent the meeting at a local diner affected their respective marriages, but by February 1943, both had obtained a divorce.[192] On February 12, 1943, Nina became the second Mrs. Charles Housden. Seven months later, Charles received a medical discharge, and the newlyweds moved to Paducah, Kentucky, near Nina's parents.

The marriage barely made it past the honeymoon phase. Nina alleged mental and physical abuse, including severe beatings that caused her to miscarry twice.

Nina would later depict Charles as a womanizer who kept a scorecard of his various affairs. He took sadistic pleasure in kissing and telling his wife all about his liaisons. If that wasn't bad enough, he would compare her performance in bed to that of his other lady friends. Despite Charles's lechery, Nina remained faithful and was floored when she learned that he had filed for divorce in February 1944—one year after they tied the knot in St. Louis.

Not one to take rejection lightly, Nina began stalking her soon-to-be ex-husband number two.

Nina may or may not have been a battered wife, but she had a violent streak. In March 1944, Charles obtained a restraining order on the basis of threats Nina had made. The following month, on April 10, Charles's sister Ruth Burkeen swore out a warrant after Nina threatened her and her mother by waving a butcher knife at them. Nina did not want Ruth and Charles's widowed mother to move to Paducah. She apparently wanted to isolate Charles from his family.

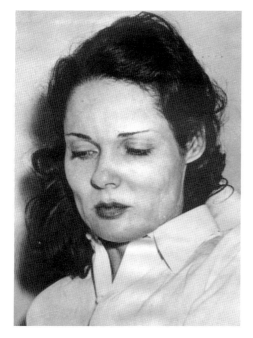

Pretty deadly: Nina Housden in a pensive moment after she confessed to the slaying of her husband. *Author's collection.*

By May 1944, Charles had had enough of the pretty yet volatile Nina. He fled Kentucky for Detroit, where he went to work as a Greyhound bus driver, but he couldn't shake Nina loose. She followed him north, rented an apartment in Highland Park, took a job as a truck driver for the American Railway Express Company and continued to dog her estranged soon-to-be ex-husband.

She would show up at the Greyhound garage and yell taunts at him. She would ride buses he drove. On one occasion, she used a taxi to pursue a bus Charles was driving. When the cab caught up to the Greyhound, Nina shouted "I'll kill you" through the open window. The harassment became so intense that Charles sought a legal remedy in October. A judge issued an injunction that barred Nina from riding in any bus driven by Charles; going to the Greyhound terminal to see him; and attempting to contact him via phone calls, letters or telegrams.

With their divorce almost finalized, Nina managed to coax Charles into going on one final date. They met at 10:30 p.m. on Monday, December 18, 1944, and went to a movie. When Nina suggested they consummate their date in her apartment, Charles didn't realize or even suspect that his ex-wife had something more sinister in mind than a goodbye tumble.

After they made love, Nina later recalled, Charles gave her notes on her performance and compared her lovemaking to other women he had known.

Charles never figured Nina as an avenging angel and never suspected foul play as she handed him a spiked glass of wine.

Nina planned to take the body back home to Kentucky, where she would inter it in a secret grave, but the new automobile she bought was not ready, so she remained in the apartment with the corpse until Wednesday.

On Wednesday, she began her final preparations for the trip south. She realized that she could never carry Charles's corpse to the car, so she decided to dismember it. Nina created a drop cloth with several layers of newspapers and a rubber sheet. Using a straight-edged razor, she sliced through the epidermis, muscle, ligaments and tendons attaching the feet to the ankles. She removed the legs at the knees and the arms at the shoulder joints. She completed the dismemberment by cutting through the neck muscles and sawing through the cervical vertebrae to separate the head from the torso. Then she washed the head in the kitchen sink. She wrapped the arms and legs in newspaper and dropped the head into a box.

She loaded the pieces onto the back seat and began the drive south, but her car broke down just outside of Toledo.

Told it would take three days to fix the engine, Nina refused to leave the car and did her best to keep prying eyes from the back seat. After two days, one of the mechanics noticed a peculiar odor emanating from the rolled-up newspapers. Nina explained that the packages contained venison she was taking south.

For forty-eight hours she kept an around-the-clock vigil broken only by an occasional catnap. By the end of the second day, Nina could not keep her eyes open. When she nodded off, one of the mechanics peeked inside the newspaper wrappings to discover a human leg.

Nina awoke to see a police officer standing over her, a pair of handcuffs dangling from his grasp.

Because investigators in both Toledo and Detroit questioned Nina Housden, she confessed twice. The opposite of tight-lipped, Nina was a voluble suspect and made several incriminating statements.

She described the killing in detail:

> *Charles was stripped down to his shorts and undershirt, and as he sat in a chair in a drunken stupor, I took a cord I used to dry my clothes on and got behind his chair.*
>
> *I got the rope around his neck, braced myself against the chair and twisted the rope until I thought he was dead. He slumped to the floor and then I went into the kitchen and went to sleep with my head in my arms on the kitchen table.*

Nina confessed to premeditation when she described previous attempts to kill Charles. "I wanted to kill him several times and I tried to poison him," she said. "My love for him was so great that I could not sleep. He had been running around with women and I could not stand that."

"Now I feel perfectly free," Nina added. "It is a great load off my mind. I have never felt better in my life. I'm sorry I didn't kill him a long time ago."[193]

"This is the first peace of mind I've had. Now I know where he is. He was my soulmate. If I were free, I would go to Kentucky and kill a couple of women he had affairs with."[194]

The flippant tone concealed the inner turmoil Nina felt after murdering and dismembering her soulmate. Deeply troubled, she tried to kill herself by stuffing paper in her mouth and nostrils.

Nina's second confession took place in the Highland Park Police Station, just across the street from the apartment where she garroted her husband and dismembered his body.

She kept her composure throughout the interview with Assistant Prosecutor Harold Helper. Her cool demeanor cracked just once, when she described how she had dismembered Charles's body.

"I was going to bury the head in a cave near Paducah, Kentucky. I intended to strew the other parts along the route," Nina explained.

Nina said that jealousy caused her to plot Charles's murder. "I knew I had to kill him because he took special pride in going out with wives of other men he met at the station," she explained. "He boasted about them and I was very jealous."[195]

She added an ominous statement that suggested she might try to cheat the hangman a second time. "It's too bad Michigan doesn't have capital punishment," she said. Afraid that Nina might make a second suicide attempt, Highland Park authorities put her under twenty-four-hour surveillance.

In both the Toledo and Highland Park confessions, Nina cast the crime as an emotional catharsis. In Toledo, she said that the murder had given her "peace of mind." In Highland Park, she described Charles's murder as the best medicine for her recurring migraines. "I had violent headaches for a year because of the way my husband treated me," Nina related to prosecuting attorney Julian G. McIntosh, "but they cleared up after I killed him."[196]

Despite the mistreatment, she loved Charles dearly. "I'm sorry he's gone," Nina lamented. "I really loved him."[197]

A first-degree murder charge was a foregone conclusion. During her two confessions, Nina made several statements that suggested premeditation. She said that Charles's demise was a year in the planning and was preceded by two earlier attempts, one of which involved a poisoned cigarette that Charles refused to smoke.

Nina Housden was evaluated and determined fit to stand trial, which took place in April 1945. Chief assistant prosecutor Frank Shemanske outlined the case for the prosecution, which was based on the theory that Nina murdered her husband because she was jealous and did not want to share her ex-husband with other women.

Nina's attorney Harry Kent likewise outlined his client's case, which was based on self-defense. The murder of Charles Housden was a preemptive strike—Nina killed him before he had the chance to kill her. It was evident from the outset that Kent's case would hinge on Nina's testimony; to make a case for self-defense, she would need to describe the abuse she suffered. She would need to be convincing. She hoped that the makeup of the jury—seven women and five men—would be an advantage, especially if one or more of the women knew a wife whose husband mistreated her.

Instead of adopting a stoic façade, Nina wept as she listened to a Toledo police officer who uncovered the ghastly secret in the backseat of her car. "She told me then," Michael Liwo testified, "that she had planned to kill her husband for over a year. The night of the murder she said she offered him a cigaret [sic] she had treated with poison. But he refused it."[198]

The proof of premeditation continued to pile up. Shemanske introduced evidence that months prior to the murder, Nina had studied how to dismember a human body.

Witnesses testified about Nina's aggressive and threatening behavior. Joseph C. Courson, a fellow bus driver, detailed an incident when Nina chased her husband in a taxi cab. "Mrs. Housden had the cab window open and was using abusive language," Courson recalled. "She threatened to keep following him and kept screaming 'I'll kill you.'"[199]

A neighbor testified that the previous October, Nina opened her purse and showed her a handgun she had acquired. Charles's landlady described two separate incidents when she heard Nina threaten to kill Charles.

With tears streaming down her cheeks, Nina catalogued the abuses she suffered at the hands of her husband when she took the stand in her own defense. He promised to give her children, she testified, but then reneged as soon as they became husband and wife.

During her turn on the stand, Nina became so emotionally distraught that Judge Frank B. Ferguson adjourned for the day.

The trial resumed on Thursday with Nina once again in the hot seat. In discussing her motive, Nina represented herself not as a cold, calculated plotter but as a mentally and physically abused woman who snapped.

"He would show me pictures of other women, and explain the strange reactions he got from each one of them," she testified. "He always bragged of what he could do with women. I did not intend to kill him that night, but I knew I would if he drove me any further with his impossible demands."[200]

During a brutal cross-examination, Schmanske elicited several damning admissions from the defendant. Nina admitted that Charles had begun divorce proceedings in March, and she admitted that Charles obtained an injunction to stop her harassment. She also said that the garroting wasn't her first attempt on Charles's life.

"I tried to kill him two or three times before, after he had beaten me," she said. "I used a butcher knife once."[201] Schmanske entered into evidence a coat perforated in several places, which Nina identified as the coat Charles wore when she attacked him with the blade.

Asked why she murdered Charles, Nina said, "Because I was afraid of him. I loved him so much that it was hell with him and hell without him."[202]

Kent attempted to call two psychologists to the stand, but Circuit Court judge Frank Ferguson wouldn't allow it. Nina had been examined prior to the trial and found to be sane, and the defense did not enter an insanity plea.

The jury deliberated for three and a half hours before returning a verdict. They found that Nina had committed premeditated murder, which carried a mandatory life sentence.

Nina's "hell without" her husband would be the Detroit House of Correction.

Nina did her time at the new Detroit House of Correction: a prison complex in Plymouth Township that replaced the aging older prison in Detroit's Fourth Ward. She had served twenty-two years when she made a deal that led to her freedom in 1967. She pleaded guilty to the lesser charge of second-degree murder, basing her amended plea on her earlier argument that she faced a kill or be killed scenario with an abusive husband. Circuit judge Nathan Kaufman accepted the plea and found Nina guilty of the lesser charge. He sentenced her to nineteen to twenty years. Since Nina had already served twenty-two, she was immediately released at the age of fifty-five.

12

THE HOUSEWIFE AND THE ORPHAN

WILLIAMSTON, 1947

Darkness enveloped them as they waited for the headlights of Frank Upton's car to appear. His shift at the Oldsmobile Forge plant ended at midnight, but two hours later he had yet to return home.

It was a long two-hour wait for sixteen-year-old Richard H. Gorman and twenty-nine-year-old Josephine Upton. Gorman, an orphan from the St. Vincent de Paul Society of Detroit, lived on a farm near Dexter. Several of his siblings boarded with the Upton family—Frank, Josephine and their three children—on a farm near Williamston.

It was twenty minutes past two o'clock on the morning of August 21 when the headlights finally appeared, cutting through the darkness as they neared the Upton farm. Hiding in a copse of bushes by the front porch, Richard gripped the hunting rifle and crouched as the car rolled to a stop with the familiar sound of gravel crunching beneath the tires. Josephine knelt next to him, a loaded shotgun by her side, just in case.

Frank Upton climbed out of the car, a lit cigarette dangling from his lips and, according to Josephine, held a knife. Richard drew a bead on the bouncing orange glow, aimed and squeezed the trigger. The bullet struck Upton in the chest, piercing his heart. "He dropped like a dead bull," Richard Gorman later recalled. He and Mrs. Upton ran to the spot, stood over the body and watched Frank Upton's chest rise, fall, rise and then fall for the last time. The tide had gone out on Frank Upton's life. Gorman jabbed the dead man's foot with the butt of the rifle just to be sure.

The gunshot woke Richard's fifteen-year-old brother Alfred, who was sleeping in the farmhouse with five other orphans from the St. Vincent de Paul Society of Detroit and the three Upton children. According to one account, he joined Richard and Josephine just in time to see Frank Upton's final respiration.[203]

Richard and Josephine rolled Upton's body in a canvas tarp and with Alfred's help loaded it into the trunk of his car. The two then drove to a dump near the Dexter farm, where Richard Gorman boarded. They scooped out a shallow cavity and covered the body with a thin veil of dirt and a layer of tin cans. "It was getting daylight," Richard remembered, "and we were afraid we would be seen so we didn't bother to cover up the body anymore, and went back to the farm and washed the blood out of the trunk of the car."[204]

Afraid that a heavy rainfall might disgorge Frank Upton's body from the shallow grave, Richard returned to the dump the next day and dug a deeper grave and covered it with a thicker layer of trash. Over the succeeding days, he would return to make sure that the dead man's body remained underground.

Upon returning from one foray, Richard reportedly told Josephine that an army of maggots had rendered the body unrecognizable. He planned to dig up the skeletonized remains the following spring and obliterate the soft bones by plowing over them when he worked the field. If all went according to plan, the shards would be turned over with the earth and become part of the landscape.[205]

He would never have the chance.

Two weeks later, the state police received a tip about Frank Upton's mysterious and uncharacteristic disappearing act in August.

The tip came from Isabel Giglac, a friend of Josephine Upton. Following the murder, Josephine told Giglac that Frank had run out on her but left the car behind. She asked for her friend's help in obtaining a job at the Fisher Body plant.

The first insinuation of foul play came when the two women met at a café the next day. After Giglac's husband came to the table and asked for some money, Josephine made an off-color remark about Isabel getting rid of her deadbeat man. Thinking Josephine's aside nothing more than a morbid joke, Isabel Giglac laughed.

Josephine admitted to killing Frank and dumping his body in Dexter but then later contradicted herself by saying that she froze, so Richard fired the fatal shot. In another telling, she indicated that Richard would admit pulling the trigger if anyone found out about it. He would say that he shot Frank Upton in self-defense.

Isabel Giglac took her story to the state police, who began an investigation.

Both Josephine Upton and Richard Gorman denied knowing anything about Frank Upton's disappearance or whereabouts. On Friday, September 5, detectives brought them in for questioning after Alfred Gorman confessed about helping the pair load a dead body into the trunk of the Upton's automobile.

The interrogations had stretched into the early hours when the first crack appeared in their stony façades. Richard Gorman broke first. When a detective asked Richard how many times Frank Upton was shot, he responded, "Only one shot was fired."[206]

A full confession followed. The boy said that he and Mrs. Upton had planned the murder as early as April because, he said, Frank Upton was a cruel man who did not make idle threats. He agreed to pull the trigger when, the day before the murder, a panicky Josephine came to the Dexter farm and told him about Upton's threat to do away with his three children and the orphans, including three of Gorman's siblings.

According to Richard, Upton made the ominous threat on August 20, but he confessed that he and Mrs. Upton began plotting the murder as early as April and planned to see it through the following November. This timeline did not indicate any urgency and did not jive with the motive that Richard provided. Nonetheless, he maintained that he shot Frank Upton to protect the children. "It had to be done." He said, "Somebody was gonna do it because he was so mean."[207]

Gorman explained that on numerous occasions, Josephine had confided in him that she wished to kill her husband but lacked the nerve. "So I decided to do it for her."[208]

"She told me she would make it right with me some day for killing her husband," Richard explained. "I told her I didn't want anything for it."[209]

Richard said he planned to live on the Dexter farm for a year and then move in the Upton residence where he could live with his siblings from the orphanage and help Mrs. Upton with the farmwork.

His repeated references to "Jo"—Josephine—hinted at a possible intimacy between the plotters. Asked about the nature of his relationship to Upham's pretty widow, Gorman denied any romantic involvement other than a single time when she kissed him on the back of the neck.[210]

Without a hint of emotion in his tone, Gorman explained that, using Upton's lit cigarette as a bull's-eye, he dropped him "like a dead bull" with one shot. He went on to describe the clandestine burial and agreed to lead investigators to the exact spot. He certainly did not appear upset by the crime. If anything, he seemed proud of his marksmanship.

Even in the hot seat, Josephine Upton was a looker. She had wavy red hair—not fire engine or brick red but a dark auburn—that she wore shoulder-length and parted on the side. Ivory, blemish-free skin contrasted with her dark hair and gave her a youthful appearance.

She was born Josephine Jury on December 25, 1916, the oldest of Williamston-area farmer Paul Jury's eight children. After graduating from Williamston High School, she married Frank Upton. She took a job as a housekeeper for a local physician until Frank got a job at an automotive plant. She spent her days managing dairy cows and children, both of which led to a monthly windfall in excess of $400.

By all accounts, the Uptons had a contentious relationship with arguments that sometimes escalated from verbal sparring to physical violence. Sometimes, Josephine retreated to her father's farm, but she always returned, ready and willing to forgive. After one particularly nasty squabble, she sought the counsel of a divorce lawyer, but it did not progress past an injunction. Josephine explained that she did not want to cause trouble for Frank—besides, he had promised to reform.

A curvaceous beauty, her weight had bloated to 232 pounds at one point. By the summer of '47, however, Josephine's figure had returned to the hourglass shape of her youth. She later attributed the drastic weight loss to the stress caused by her husband's abuse, but a steady diet of medicine and cigarettes helped.[211]

Confronted with Gorman's complete confession, Josephine Upton admitted everything. Unlike her youthful partner, emotion overwhelmed her as she told of the plot, the murder and the unceremonious burial of her husband under a pile of garbage. Often pausing to stifle her sobs, she expressed remorse that she hadn't divorced her husband. "I wish now it had been me rather than him," she sobbed.

For Richard Gorman, the murder was a way to protect his siblings from being sent back to the orphanage; for Josephine, it was a matter of self-preservation. She depicted Frank Upton as a sadistic tyrant who sometimes put a knife to her throat and threatened to cut her from ear to ear. She denied any intimacies with the youngster, although she did admit that she secreted the teenager in the attic on more than one occasion, and insisted that she plotted her husband's demise not to make way for "Dick" but because she believed that Frank planned to murder her and the children.

The day before the murder, Josephine explained, her husband savagely beat their ten-year-old son because he had a mishap with the tractor and then throttled her before threatening to do away with the children and send the foster kids back to Detroit. Frightened, she raced to Dexter and told Richard about Frank's threats. Richard returned to the Upham place.

"We just sat there talking—Dick and I—at home that evening," she explained. "I told him how he [Frank] had beaten Carl that morning and how he threatened to get rid of my kids."

Josephine realized that the crime had ruined sixteen-year-old Richard Gorman and exclaimed, "It was all my fault. I'm old enough to be those kids' mother."[212]

Investigators escorted Josephine and Richard to the trash heap where they had concealed the body. The entourage arrived at about forty thirty on the morning of Saturday, September 6, 1947.

Richard stood at the base of a tin-can pyramid and pointed to the spot where they would find Frank Upton. His narrow shoulders, long neck and wiry torso made his clothes—a blue shirt and denim overalls—appear too big for his body. His close-cropped hair accentuated his ears, making them appear to jut outward.

After some spade work, the crew managed to unearth the badly decomposing remains of Frank Upton.

The trial took place in December. Both Josephine and Richard faced first-degree murder charges and possible life sentences.

Prosecuting attorney Charles R. MacLean countered the self-defense theory by providing an alternative motive: the twenty-nine-year-old housewife had fallen for her codefendant, and Frank Upton stood in the way of her warped fantasy of a happier-ever-after with Richard.

He read a letter Josephine had penned to Richard.

Using terms of endearment such as "Dearest Dick" and "loads of love," the letter had all the tones of a love letter. "You know I love you and Al[fred Gorman] one hell of a lot," Josephine wrote. "Al says you are coming home for good after deer season. Are you going to?" Josephine asked. "Do you think it is safe quite so soon? I want you home so badly but let's play it safe—what do you think?"

The letter concluded, "I'll be so glad when we are started on our easy street and you can come home for keeps," she added. "I think lots of you even if I don't write too often." She closed with "Loads of love, Al, Jo and family."[213]

Some of the most damaging testimony came from the lips of Josephine through the proxy of witnesses who testified to hearing her make some provocative statements that undermined her guise as a battered housewife. She bragged about chasing Frank into the woods with a shotgun, asked if a gasoline-fueled explosion in his car would obliterate all trace of foul play and declared that she had purchased wine to share with the boys.

Josephine took the stand and characterized Frank as an oversexed, heavy-drinking ogre with a zipper problem and a bad temper. Without her husband to contradict her, she catalogued the abuses she allegedly suffered at his oversized hands, which included beating her, choking her until she lost consciousness, firing a gun in her direction, lashing her and her children with a garden hose, pressing a knife to her throat and dragging her into the bedroom and taking her against her will. On one occasion, she said she woke up to find one of Frank's conquests in bed next to her. She contemplated divorce and even consulted an attorney but changed her mind after Frank promised to reform. Despite it all, she still loved him, even in the minutes before Richard shot him.

She contradicted Richard's earlier statements by denying that the two had planned the crime months in advance. In an attempt to cast the shooting as an act of self-defense rather than a cold-blooded, premeditated murder, Josephine explained that that afternoon, Frank threatened to kill her and the children when he returned from work. She believed him, and the knife she found next to his body after Richard shot him seemed to support his intention to make good on the threat.

"I owe my life and those of all my children to Dick," she testified.[214]

During his cross-examination, prosecutor Charles R. MacLean did his best to expose contradictions and discrepancies in Josephine's testimony and present a face other than the soft-spoken damsel in distress guise that the defendant had adopted. He scored points with the jury when Josephine admitted to having a sharp temper that sometimes led to physical altercations with Frank. MacLean asked her if she used cord to whip her children, but she said she used a belt instead.

When asked if she had crossed the line with Dick, she responded, "I have never been unfaithful to my husband," and vehemently denied having a secret affair with the teenager.[215] She admitted, however, to secreting Richard in the attic after her husband accused her of infidelity and demanded that Richard leave and never return.

With a brutal line of questions, MacLean succeeded in prying several damaging admissions from Josephine's lips. As she watched from her covert in the bushes, Frank waltzed right past her and she did not utter a peep, effectively sending her husband to his doom.

"You let him go to his death didn't you?" MacLean asked.

"If Dick missed," Josephine replied, "I was to kill him—I mean shoot him."

When MacLean asked, "You drafted Richard, didn't you?" she replied, "Yes."

Dick followed Josephine to the stand. Those hoping to see a cathartic moment of remorse left the courtroom disappointed. Responding to questions with the same emotionless, deadpan expression he wore when he confessed to ambushing Frank Upton and keeping a vigil over his remains, he appeared more like a cardboard cutout than the defendant in a murder trial. His stony demeanor may have harmed more than helped his defense; he appeared more of a puppet than a martyr.

His responses during MacLean's cross-examination indicated a total lack of remorse.

"I think I was right [in shooting Frank Upton]," he admitted and said that he would do it again "under the same circumstances."

MacLean confronted the witness with his confession and asked about specific admissions, such as planning the murder for November, that tended to show premeditation. Gorman said he had lied and denounced that statement as the product of fear and coercion.

The prosecutor called a series of witnesses whose testimony suggested that something was rotten at the Upton place; that home was not where the Uptons' heart was. This testimony indicated that both Frank and Josephine were heavy-handed with their children, their foster children and each other.

Nine-year-old Jimmy Broomfield, one of the orphans living at the Upton farm, both helped and hurt the defense when he testified to receiving rubber-hose floggings from both Mr. and Mrs. Upton. Mrs. Upton, he said, once burned his tongue as a punishment for swearing. He pointed to a scar below his eye that he got when Frank Upton tripped him and he fell on a rock.

The boy also told of seeing Frank Upton beating and choking Josephine. One beating took place in the front yard, when Frank knocked Josephine unconscious, "like when you lay down and go to sleepytown," he said. Another incident came after Josephine needled Frank by declaring that he would not down an entire plateful of potatoes and eggs. After Frank won the bet, he choked Josephine.[216]

Two other orphans, teenagers lodged in the Upton house, testified to receiving beatings at the hands of Frank Upham and witnessing him knocking around Josephine. One of the boys said that Josephine Upham had given them alcohol on more than one occasion.

One of Josephine's sisters told a hair-raising story of a gun-toting Frank Upton marching Josephine from the house by gunpoint. She took her sister to a divorce lawyer, and Frank responded to the injunction with a litany of expletives and an ominous threat to get even with his wife.

Josephine's father, Paul Jury, told of numerous attempts to broker a peace between the feuding spouses and recalled one incident when Josephine came to him with half of her face black and blue.

This testimony went a long way toward showing the victim as an oversized bullyboy with a hair-trigger temper, but no one recalled hearing Frank Upton threaten to kill either Josephine or any of the children. No one, that is, except Josephine.

The self-defense claim would hinge on her testimony and her testimony alone. It would be her voice that would either liberate the defendants or send them to prison for life.

The jury was presented two opposite and conflicting portrayals of Josephine Upton: the prosecution's version of a vixen who carried on with a sixteen-year-old orphan and then used him as a tool to dispose of her husband, or the defense version of a battered housewife who conspired to kill her sadistic husband to protect herself and the ten children in her care.

The self-defense defense fell apart under scrutiny. The two defendants had not contacted the police after Frank Upton's alleged threats. No amount of rhetoric or victim-blaming would change that fact. Even at the last minute, when Josephine could have warned Frank or asked Dick to stand down, she remained mute. On the contrary, she averred, "If Dick missed, I was to kill him—I mean shoot him."

The jury preferred to see Josephine Upton as a villain and Richard Gorman as her willing accomplice.

After the trial, the now-convicted murderers said their goodbyes before going their separate ways. The semiprivate moment took place in the matron's office at the police department. Reporters could watch from a distance, but what the two whispered to each other would remain unheard.

It is difficult to know just what happened behind closed doors of the Upton house. Why would an impressionable sixteen-year-old agree to commit a cold-blooded, premediated murder? His actions after the shooting—butting Upham with the rifle—suggest a deep animosity, but where did this hatred originate?

If there was any truth to Josephine's characterization of Frank Upton as a vicious tyrant, the youngster may not have needed much, if any, prodding, especially if he had witnessed Frank's cruelty in person. During his interrogation, Richard Gorman characterized Upton as "mean all the time," but added a clarifier: "He seemed to get meaner that day." "That day" referred to Frank Upton's alleged beating of his ten-year-old son and threats to get rid of the children and ship the orphans down the river—threats that Gorman heard secondhand through the filter of Josephine Upton.

On the other hand, if Richard had not seen Frank Upton's Hyde in action, he may have needed some coaxing, which may have come in one of several forms. A few well-placed comments or insinuations that suggested the kids were not safe may have triggered Gorman's sense of self-preservation. Or Josephine may have attacked the youth with a constant barrage of hearsay threats that convinced him of the need for extreme action. During interrogation, he said that she had expressed her desire to kill her husband on several occasions but lacked the courage. Undoubtedly, she also told him about Frank's alleged habit of putting a knife to her throat.

Did Josephine Upton play the role of damsel in distress and appeal to the Sir Galahad in every sixteen-year-old boy? Did she make promises in the dark? Or did she use more direct means to stimulate his sense of chivalry?

One particular comment undercut the notion that the crime was motivated by an urgent sense of self-preservation. Richard said that they had planned Frank Upton's demise as early as April, and Josephine indicated that the hit was intended to take place in November. The time lapse indicates that the pair did not feel that the victim posed an imminent threat and that something other than the August 20 rant motivated Frank Upton's murder.

That Richard Herman "Dick" Gorman pulled the trigger was never in doubt, but why remains a tantalizing mystery. "The story behind his role in the slaying," noted a *Lansing State Journal* reporter following the conviction, "has never been brought to light and will go to prison with both him and Mrs. Upton."[217]

Whatever secrets they kept, the two convicted killers took them to the grave.

Richard H. Gorman served seventeen years of his life sentence, leaving prison on parole in 1965. He died in 1998 at the age of sixty-seven. His former foster mother, Josephine Marie Upton, left the House of Correction on parole in 1966. She died in Charlotte in 2007 at the age of eighty-nine.

13

THE BARK IS WORSE THAN THE BITE

PONTIAC, 1984

Carol Ege has the dubious dishonor of being convicted for murder—the same murder—twice. The odd story of a love triangle and a hotly contested bite mark identification took over two decades to reach a conclusion.

A week after Valentine's Day in 1984, Oakland County residents were horrified by news of the Ripper-esque slaying of Cindy Thompson, who was seven months pregnant at the time. In the early morning hours of February 22, Thompson's former boyfriend Mark Davis stumbled upon the grisly scene in the bedroom of the home Thompson rented on Seneca Street—a quiet, tree-lined neighborhood in Pontiac. Davis ran to a friend's house and asked him to call the police, who arrived on the scene within minutes of receiving the call.

She had been bludgeoned several times in the head with a hammer-like object, stabbed multiple times in the neck and upper chest, slashed in the right side and partially disemboweled. The body lay on its left side in a pool of blood with a pile of organs spilling out of the crescent-shaped gash running from her spine to her midsection.

The forensic evidence indicated a frenzied attack. One thrust with an edged weapon was so powerful, it severed Thompson's spinal cord and possibly bent the tip of the blade when it struck bone. Another stab wound to the uterus had severed the oxygen supply to the fetus.

A patch of dried blood and a clump of hair at the base of the stairs leading to the second-story bedroom indicated that the perpetrator either began the savage attack there and chased (or dragged) the terrified victim to the bedroom or trailed blood from the murder scene when leaving. There was no evidence of forced entry, and the back door was found unlocked, so the killer may have crept into the house from the rear entry. Alternately, Thompson may have unwittingly admitted the killer when she answered a knock at the front door.

Cindy Thompson's movements helped establish a time frame for her murder as sometime after 9:00 p.m. on February 21 and before 1:00 a.m. on February 22.[218]

Cindy Thompson spent the last day of her life babysitting for the couple who lived across the street and from whom she rented the Seneca Street home. After the job ended at approximately 8:00 p.m., she went to her landlady's place of employment and visited for about an hour. She left, presumably to return home, between 8:45 p.m. and 9:15 p.m. A neighbor later reported hearing a car pull into the driveway sometime around 9:00 p.m. followed by a second car that left a short time later. A friend tried to phone Thompson between 8:00 and 9:00 p.m., but the line was busy, perhaps because at that instant, Thompson was in a desperate life-or-death struggle with her as-yet unmasked killer.

During the initial investigation, an interesting cast of characters emerged, including Davis's live-in girlfriend Carol Ege. Davis, who discovered the body, had had an ongoing relationship with Ege that stretched back to the late 1970s. He also had a romantic relationship with Cindy Thompson. He would later state in court that he believed he was the father of Thompson's baby and planned to move out of Ege's home and move in with Cindy Thompson instead. He also believed that Ege knew about his relationship with Thompson.[219]

Ege's animosity with the deceased had bubbled to the surface several times in the preceding months, including one physical altercation during which she pushed Thompson down a flight of steps, and she tried to finagle an alibi for the time of Thompson's murder.

Carol Ege was a promising suspect with a viable motive, but investigators found no physical evidence placing her at the crime scene. By the end of 1984, the case had become cold.

Eight years later, the Thompson case thawed when detectives received information about a possible piece of evidence connecting Carol Ege with the murder. One of Ege's former boyfriends, with whom she lived sometime in 1984 or 1985, found a knife with a bent tip in a box Ege packed when they split up. The blade was streaked with what looked like dried blood and "gristle." He put the knife in a dishwasher, but then, suspecting the knife was possibly used in the murder, contacted the police. He subsequently turned over a box containing three hammers that also supposedly belonged to Ege.

The Cindy Thompson murder case was reopened in 1993. Oakland County authorities sent evidence gathered at the crime scene to the state police crime lab for a fresh look. Forensic experts examined the physical evidence and conducted DNA tests but found nothing tying Carol Ege to the bloodbath in Cindy Thompson's bedroom.

The knife with the bent tip was also a dead end. Although consistent with the neck wound that severed Thompson's spinal cord, the blade did not contain any traces of blood, possibly because its finder washed it before realizing its possible connection to the case.

The link needed to make a case against Ege would surface when investigators conducted an exhumation of Thompson's remains. The disinterment resulted from what appeared to be discrepancies between the autopsy photographs and autopsy report. A review revealed several instances in which wounds apparent in the photographs were not noted on the report, so it was decided to reexamine the remains.

The coffin disgorged a secret that had lain six feet under for the better part of a decade: what some believed was a previously unidentified bite mark on Thompson's left cheek.

During the 1984 autopsy, the mark on Thompson's cheek was classified as livor mortis or the blue-purple, bruise-like blotches that form when, in the absence of a heartbeat, blood pools wherever gravity takes it. In crime scene investigation, livor mortis is a telltale sign of the body's position at the time the heart stopped and can indicate if the body had been moved postmortem. In the case of Cindy Thompson, the livor mortis suggested that she died lying on her left side, as she was found.

The alleged bite mark, if it was a bite mark, supposedly matched Carol Ege's dentition and was therefore the long-sought piece of physical evidence, albeit a hotly contested one, connecting Ege with the crime scene. A murder indictment quickly followed.

The trial opened in December 1993 in Oakland County Circuit Court. The prosecution forwarded a theory depicting Ege as an obsessive, jealous lover who stood in one corner of a love triangle and brutally murdered her competition. The evidence came in three parts: threatening statements Ege supposedly made in the days leading up the murder, past verbal and physical altercations with Thompson and the bite mark.

As the only physical evidence placing Ege at the crime scene, the bite mark was the linchpin in the prosecution's case. A forensic dentist testified that the bite mark came from the mouth of Carol Ege with a probability that he calculated at 3.5 million to one.[220]

The bite mark ostensibly proved that Carol Ege murdered Cindy Thompson, and her own loose lips illustrated the dark persona capable of savagely knifing and slashing a pregnant woman.

Over the unsuccessful motions of the defense, a parade of witnesses testified to hearing Ege make some threatening statements about Cindy Thompson and her unborn baby. She made overtures about hiring someone to kill Thompson. She said she wanted to slash Thompson's throat. She made an ominous prediction that Thompson's love child would never be born.

Anecdotes from the witness stand illustrated a propensity toward violent, retributive acts.

In a rage-fueled frenzy, she tore apart some T-shirts that Thompson gifted Mark Davis for his birthday. In December 1983, Ege assaulted Thompson, who was five months pregnant, and pushed her down a staircase. Ege later claimed that she wanted Thompson to miscarry.

One of the more damaging voices against Carol Ege at the trial came from Carol Ege herself through statements she allegedly made to a roommate. She offered free rent in exchange for an alibi; she attempted to contract a hitman and supposedly boasted about going to the bank to take out money for the hit. She subsequently tore her bankbook into shreds, stuffed them into an empty milk carton and tossed the carton in a dumpster.

Ege's defense countered by pointing out that Ege was at home during the time frame established for the murder, and none of the prosecution's witnesses could say otherwise. Mark Davis testified that Ege was home all that night, and Ege's other roommate was at work until 3:00 a.m.

Piece by piece, Ege's defense challenged the prosecution's so-called evidence.

The bite mark—the only physical evidence placing Ege at the crime scene—was not a bite mark but a patch of livor mortis as it was originally classified in 1984. Since Thompson died while leaning on her left side, pooling blood caused the livor mortis on her left cheek that was later mistaken for a bite mark. The purplish splotch was like a Rorschach ink blot, and investigators had in essence interpreted it in a way that fit their theory of the crime.

To prove the claim that the crimson blotch had been misinterpreted, the defense called two medical professionals who had conducted an independent review of the evidence and declared the spot nothing more than livor mortis left by nature's physical processes and not by Thompson's frenzied attacker. One of the experts—a dentist as well as a medical doctor—testified that even if it were a bite mark, it would not match Ege's pattern of teeth.

And several of the prosecution witnesses were onetime suspects and not the most trustworthy of people. In its 1996 review of the case, the Michigan Appeals Court noted, "Many of the prosecution's witnesses, other than police officers and experts…were impeached on the stand with prior testimony or statements. At the time of the murder, most of the witnesses drank heavily and used drugs."[221]

Further, Carol Ege's alleged threats were not threats but harmless angst. She didn't like her rival in the love triangle, and this animosity naturally found expression in hollow statements that the prosecution had presented as precursors to murder.

As for evidence that Ege paid for a hit on Thompson, a detective testified that he attempted to follow the money trail but could not locate the bank. Ege's boast of paying a hitman was just another insubstantial bit of whimsy or at worst wishful thinking.

Testifying in her own defense, Ege denied everything. Responding to questions by the prosecution, she admitted to aborting two of her own pregnancies, one that resulted from her relationship with Davis. The defense did not object to the line of questions, which the prosecution proposed as evidence that Ege's conscience would not prevent her from killing an unborn fetus.

The trial ended in January 1994 with a verdict of guilty. Barring a successful appeal, Carol Ege was headed to prison for life without the possibility of parole.

In 1996, the Michigan Court of Appeals reviewed the case and found no reversible errors in the trial records, although it did characterize the questions about Ege's abortions as "irresponsible."[222] In the decision, the court acknowledged that the alleged bite mark was the only physical clue tying Ege to the murder.[223]

"This is a troubling case," the justices noted. "The crime is horrific. The initial investigation was deficient. Defendant was not charged until nine years after the murder. There are others who are logical suspects. No one saw defendant at the scene the evening of the murder. No physical evidence links defendant to the crime except testimony that a mark on the victim's cheek is a bite mark that is highly consistent with defendant's dentition."[224]

And that contested piece of evidence would be dismissed.

Almost a decade after the gavel came down on Carol Ege, a U.S. Court of Appeals ordered her release based on the forensic dentist's testimony about the alleged bite mark, which the federal court ruled unreliable, inadmissible and highly prejudicial to the jury.

By the time of the federal court decision in July 2005, the same dentist's bite mark testimony in five felony cases had come under fire. All five defendants subsequently received new trials. When Carol Ege became the sixth to win a new trial, two of the defendants—convicted rapists—had already been acquitted.[225] While Oakland County authorities decried the court's decision, basing their objection on the other evidence tending to prove Ege's guilt, the forty-eight-year-old prepared for a second go in court.

Most the characters from the first trial gathered in the Oakland County Circuit Court when the second trial opened in October 2007. It was a virtual carbon copy of the first, minus the bite mark evidence. For a second time, Carol Ege was convicted of first-degree murder and sentenced to life in prison.

She apologized to the family of the victim but insisted she had nothing to do with the murder. "I do pray to God," she added. "He will be our judge. I didn't not kill Cindy Thompson."[226]

Ege's second conviction led to a second appeal, based partly on the contention that without the bite mark evidence, her conviction rested on a foundation of wholly circumstantial evidence. She also questioned the legality of testimony regarding the bent-tipped knife.

Once again, the appeals court reviewed the case and once again affirmed the verdict. Addressing the circumstantial evidence objection, the justices concluded, "Although each link in the prosecution's chain of proof against defendant is circumstantial, the conjoined references flowing from the evidence are neither speculative nor irrational, and therefore permit a jury to reasonably conclude beyond a reasonable doubt that defendant committed the murder."[227]

As for the knife evidence, the court concluded that testimony linked the blade to Ege, and the forensic testimony offered at the trial—that the force of a knife striking the cervical vertebrae could damage the tip in a similar fashion as the knife offered into evidence—linked the knife to the murder. The question as to whether or not Ege wielded the weapon was for the jury to answer.[228]

And they answered the question, for a second time, by convicting Carol Ege of murder.

Carol Ege, prisoner no. 235484, is currently serving life without the possibility of parole at the Women's Huron Valley Correctional Facility in Ypsilanti.

14

TWISTED FAIRY TALE

ROYAL OAK, 1984

On the evening of March 12, 1984, sixty-three-year-old widower and retired laborer Paul Lingnau had just celebrated his birthday with his brother Arthur and Arthur's wife at a Troy-area lounge. Just after 10:00 p.m., they dropped him off at his apartment complex, watching from the parking lot as he slid the key into the lock and opened the door.

Then Paul suddenly dropped to the floor. Arthur raced to the spot and found his brother lying in a pool of blood. Paul had been shot at point-blank range five times with a .45 automatic, execution-style. Five slugs to the head and chest.

It had all the hallmarks of a professional hit. The shooter did not pause to take mementoes or attempt to make it look like a robbery by snatching Lingnau's wallet. Except for a few eyewitnesses who reported seeing a man race across the parking lot and speed away in a compact car, police had no leads.

In the days before his murder, Paul Lingnau, a sixty-three-year-old widower and retired laborer from Royal Oak, made an offhand remark about someone gunning for him. He asked the apartment manager to change the locks on the front door of his apartment. Known as a quiet, reserved man, Lingnau was well-liked throughout the apartment complex. Yet clearly, something had spooked him.

Lingnau did have one enemy—Debra Lynn Edwards—who was once his sweetheart.

Their love story had all the elements of a pulp romance novel: lonely widower, deflated from years alone, met a much younger vixen—at twenty-five, young enough to be his granddaughter. She probably did not mention that she was a longtime drug user with a conviction for narcotics possession, although she may have said something about it to elicit sympathy points.

They began to spend more and more time together, and he appeared mentally and physically invigorated with the companionship of a woman almost forty years his junior. Yet he had doubts. When she suggested they make it official and exchange vows, he asked her what such a young, vibrant woman would see in an old coot like him. With tears rolling down her cheeks, she told him she loved him. It was as simple as that.

It was a reassuring response. For Paul Lingnau, her tears offered the promise of sincerity. He could scarcely believe it when she told him that she was carrying their love child.

He suspected nothing when she sweet-talked him into adding her name to a money market account worth $10,000. He suspected nothing when she moved into his apartment. She said she would take care of everything; she would cook meals for him and clean his apartment. She would pay the bills, which would be easier if he signed over his pension and social security checks. She even coaxed him into signing his car over to her. She later reported the car stolen and attempted to cash in on the insurance policy.

Three days after moving in—in early January 1984—Debra Lynn Edwards moved out, taking with her $20,000 of Lingnau's money: two checks and the money market, which she emptied. The nine-month-long fairy-tale romance had become a nightmare.

Stinging, Lingnau filed a complaint with the local police. On probation from a previous narcotics conviction and now facing an embezzlement charge, Debra Lynn Edwards was in big trouble, but the embezzlement case died with Paul Lingnau—the sole witness against her.

The timing was a little too convenient: the arrest warrant on the embezzlement charge was issued on March 9. Paul Lingnau was set to testify on March 14. He was murdered on March 12. Dead men tell no tales of a con game.

This powerful motive—along with Edwards's multiple attempts to fabricate an alibi—made her a prime suspect in the murder. Investigators, however, lacked the solid link needed to place either Edwards or one of her acquaintances in Lingnau's apartment when he arrived home that fateful evening. It would later come out that Edwards did not exactly remain mute about her role in the crime and made several seemingly damning statements, but in 1984, witnesses were reluctant to come forward.

Edwards's legal trouble did not entirely disappear with Lingnau's demise; she still faced a charge of "obtaining money by false pretenses," which stemmed from the bogus police report she filed for Lingnau's "stolen" automobile. But apart from a strong motive and some provocative speculation about a possible murder-for-hire, there was nothing connecting Edwards with Lingnau's murder.

Debra Edwards may have gotten away with murder for the time being, but she did not emerge squeaky-clean from the Lingnau affair. Convicted of "obtaining money by false pretenses," she received a sentence of five to twenty. She was on parole when she was caught in possession of cocaine, which led to another stretch behind bars.

The Lingnau murder was a decade-old cold case when a breakthrough occurred in 1994.

In 1994, Randy Rasnick—a male acquaintance of Debra Edwards (now known as Debra Starr)—attacked Starr's stepfather Argil Dennis as he convalesced with ALS in the Allen Park VA Hospital. In a savage and frenzied assault, Rasnick jabbed Dennis eighteen times with an icepick. Somehow, Dennis survived.

Arrested, Rasnick ratted out Debra Starr and her mother, Betty Dennis, for arranging the attempted hit. Rasnick told authorities a sordid story of meeting Starr at a crack house. Later, mother and daughter paid him $2,000 to murder Betty's invalid husband. Betty wanted Argil out of the way because he represented a threat to a plot that was eerily similar to Starr's bilking of Paul Lingnau. Playing the role of a recent divorcée, Betty Dennis seduced and bigamously married an elderly man in order to pilfer his life savings. But Argil—still legally her spouse—refused to play along.

Debra had an even more sinister motive for wanting her stepfather out of the picture. Argil Dennis owned a .45 automatic, which he said went missing sometime around the murder of Paul Lingnau. Investigators would later find eyewitnesses who saw Debra in possession of what appeared to be a .45 automatic. An image began to materialize of a vengeful slayer who ordered the hit on Paul Lingnau to sidestep an embezzlement charge and then ordered the hit on her stepfather to cover up her connection with the murder weapon.

Argil Dennis was a twice-marked man.

At Betty Dennis's trial in January 1990, Wayne County assistant prosecuting attorney Douglas Baker characterized the mother-daughter duo as more "life threatening" to Argil Dennis than the disease afflicting him.[229]

Rasnick—the weapon in the intended Argil Dennis hit—received fifteen to twenty; Betty Dennis, life; Starr, fifteen to thirty.

Starr was behind bars when investigators managed to gather enough evidence to charge her with Lingnau's murder in 1998—fourteen years after the fact. A grand jury, which could compel testimony, summoned witnesses who told of Debra Edwards blabbing about planning Lingnau's execution. The witness list included dozens of names, suggesting that Starr had had very loose lips. Over the ensuring decade, she talked plenty about the plot. "She did not keep quiet about this," noted Oakland County assistant prosecutor John Pietrofesa.[230]

The most damning words came from the lips of Debra Starr, as channeled through a series of witnesses who heard her making one or more incriminating statements. Starr apparently admitted to conspiring with a former boyfriend to make the hit and boasted of sending the .45 to the bottom of the Detroit River. She even bragged to a cellmate about her role in the fourteen-year-old slaying.

The witnesses rehashed their grand jury testimony in the Oakland County Circuit Court, where now forty-year-old Debra Lynn Starr faced a first-degree murder charge as "an aider and abettor" and the prospect of a life sentence, which meant that she would spend the rest of her natural life in prison.

The prosecution argued that the defendant plotted Lingnau's murder to avoid prison and then plotted her stepfather's demise to prevent him from linking her to the murder weapon. Two former boyfriends testified that Starr offered them money to murder Dennis, but they refused.[231]

On March 11, 1999—one day shy of fifteen years after Paul Lingnau's murder—the jury found Debra Lynn Starr guilty as charged. She is serving a life sentence without the possibility of parole at the Huron Valley Correctional facility. Her mother, Betty Dennis, died in 2014 at the age of eighty-one.

Starr's conviction brought partial closure to the Lingnau murder case, but one very big question remains. Who pulled the trigger?

According to testimony offered at the trial, Debra Starr allegedly bragged about having Lingnau murdered and identified the shooter by name, but authorities never managed to build a prosecutable case against anyone other than Debra Lynn Starr.

Prisoner no. 179036 is currently serving life without the possibility of parole at the Women's Huron Valley Correctional Facility.

15

BAD THINGS HAPPEN IN THREES

WAYLAND, 1990

At a little after six thirty on the morning of September 25, 1990, Wayland police officers, responding to a desperate 911 call, arrived at the Wayland home of Merilee Causley, where her daughter Diane Spencer and Spencer's five-month-old son Aaron lived. Spencer told the emergency operator that Aaron had stopped breathing, and when the officers entered the house, they found her attempting to resuscitate the boy.

Yet his skin tone was cyanotic, suggesting that he may have died sometime—perhaps hours—before the call. The key to solving the mystery of Aaron Spencer's death lay deep in his mother's psyche.

Born Diane McKay on October 23, 1967, Diane Spencer grew up in the quiet, conservative west Michigan community of Zeeland, known for farms and churches. Her early biography largely consisted of journal entries completed during various stints of drug rehab. It began with sloe gin at age twelve.[232] It all went downhill from there: marijuana, cocaine, speed, methamphetamines, LSD. She began to self-harm and frequently ran away from home. The downward spiral, she would later claim, was an attempt to cope with sexual abuse.[233]

She was attractive but mercurial, later characterized as a Jekyll-and-Hyde type whose mood could change from pleasant to sullen and spiteful in the drop of a hat.[234] She also despised confrontation. Her mother, Merilee, characterized Diane as people-pleaser who "would take the blame for anything rather than rock the boat."[235]

The troubled teenager attended Zeeland High School for a short time, but she wound up in a string of youth homes. Just before her fifteenth birthday, Diane ran away and drifted for a while. During this nomadic period, she met a truck driver who took her home to Clearfield County, Pennsylvania. They eventually moved into an apartment together.

Diane Spencer lived in a partially fictitious world. She lied about her age, saying she was nineteen when in fact she was fifteen. She said her life was in danger and claimed that someone had slid threatening notes under her door. She told people her mother had come to visit when her mother did not even know where her daughter lived.

At age fifteen, Diane gave birth to Joyce Denochick. Tragically, the infant died six weeks later, on August 6, 1983. According to Spencer, Joyce had stopped breathing.

Her death was attributed to sudden infant death syndrome. Typically, SIDS victims are less than a year in age and suffocate while sleeping, which sometimes happens when they roll over in soft bedding. Lacking the strength to raise their heads or turn over, they remain trapped in a prone position and suffocate. SIDS is a diagnosis of exclusion used when an investigation, including an autopsy, reveals no other cause of death. In the case of Joyce Denochick, however, no autopsy was conducted. Diane was asked if she wanted one, but she declined.

In 1984, seventeen-year-old Diane gave birth to another child and put the baby up for adoption, although she told at least one person that the baby died in a car wreck.[236]

At eighteen, she married Don Spencer while they were both incarcerated in the Clearfield County Jail. A year later, the couple welcomed a daughter, but history would repeat itself on September 21, 1987, when Autumn Dawn Spencer died at just fifteen days old. She had apparently stopped breathing while lying in her crib. An internal examination revealed no evidence of physical trauma. Once again, her death was attributed to SIDS.

By 1990, Diane Spencer was back in Michigan, where she would give birth to, and lose, a fourth child. Aaron Avery was the product of a relationship that began at a Narcotics Anonymous meeting after Diane had moved back home.

A rerun of Autumn Dawn's tragic and untimely death would air in Wayland. Aaron, like his half sisters before him, apparently suffered from some mysterious physical ailment. Diane repeatedly took him to doctors with complaints of flu-like symptoms and apnea events. On one occasion when Aaron had apparently stopped breathing, officers found Diane administering CPR.

After Aaron's death, Diane moved out of her mother's home and began using again, which landed her in a detoxification center where she wrote a twelve-page autobiography. The loss of yet another child sent Diane Spencer over the edge. "He was my entire world," she said. "The thought of my son is always there, the pain is ever-present. I started doing dope again the night of his funeral."[237]

An autopsy revealed no signs of disease. Aaron's lungs, however, contained the tiny petechial hemorrhages that can result from a suffocation.[238]

Investigators discovered a strange backstory to Aaron's untimely demise. In the months before Aaron's death, his mother had consulted with physicians about his supposed sleep apnea. Despite running hundreds of tests, doctors could find nothing wrong with the boy—no physiological cause for his breathing problem—but one caretaker walked in on a strange scene of Diane attempting to tinker with the hospital's monitoring equipment. She also appeared to do the exact opposite of what the doctors suggested and, in one instance, unplugged a monitor from the wall.

Spencer's bizarre behavior raised suspicions about her mental state. She was informed about a syndrome called Munchhausen by proxy and offered counseling but steadfastly refused.

Munchhausen syndrome by proxy is a factitious disorder named after Baron Hieronymus Karl Friedrich, Freiherr von Münchhausen, who delighted in spinning exaggerated yarns about his past. Someone suffering from the disorder, typically a mother, thrives on medical attention she receives through her proxy, usually her child. To obtain the coveted attention, she will create symptoms for her child. She might, for example, feed her son an emetic to create influenza symptoms. Or she might fabricate apnea events by smothering and reviving him.

Aaron Spencer was prescribed with an apnea monitor. About the size of a purse, the rectangular, box-like device contained suction cups placed on the subject to monitor heartbeat. If an event occurred, an alarm, loud enough to wake someone in another room, would sound.

According to Diane Spencer, the first apnea monitor did not function properly. She took Aaron back to the hospital because, she said, he continued to suffer from periodic seizures and apnea episodes. After this hospital stay, the physicians prescribed a second apnea monitor. This time, Diane was asked to keep a diary in which she was supposed to record when the monitor alarm sounded.

This monitor had a memory chip. Diane Spencer supposedly did not know about the memory chip, but she had evidently tampered with the device; it was missing five screws—two from one of the ends and three from the other. After Aaron's death, the device had been returned to the medical supply company, where investigators took possession of what would become a smoking-gun piece of evidence.

The printout of the chip's memory for the morning of September 25 revealed a chilling chronicle of the final minutes in Aaron Spencer's short life. At 4:49 a.m., the monitor was turned off. About a half hour later, it was turned back on, but the readout indicated no heart activity. During the next few minutes, it was turned off, on, off and on again. There was no heart activity during any of the "on" periods.

It was almost as if someone had used the monitor to determine if the boy was dead or alive, which did not align with Spencer's frantic 911 call or her story of finding Aaron not breathing.

While investigators gathered evidence, Spencer checked herself into a drug rehabilitation program. She graduated from the program on December 5 and promptly relapsed into using.

On December 10, Diane awoke around 10:00 a.m. "I stayed at the apartment where I was staying at and got high all day," she later recalled. "That was normal at that point in my life, unfortunately."[239]

That afternoon, she returned to the detoxification center to visit with a friend. While there, investigators arrested her on an uttering and publishing charge arising from writing bad checks. They transported her to the state police headquarters in Lansing, where she would undergo questioning.

The interview began around 8:00 p.m. and stretched into the early morning hours of December 11. At three hours into the five-and-a-half-hour interview, she confessed to smothering her two daughters in Pennsylvania. Joyce and Autumn Dawn had not died from SIDS, as originally thought. Rather, she suffocated Joyce with a towel and Autumn with a blanket.

By placing her own palm over her mouth and nose, Spencer demonstrated how she smothered Joyce. She intended to kill her daughter, she admitted, although she added that Joyce still had a heartbeat and later died in the hospital. She killed Autumn Dawn in a similar manner.

Spencer admitted to a third murder when she described pressing a pillow over Aaron's face. She said she tried desperately to resuscitate him and used the apnea monitor to determine if he had a pulse—an explanation that tallied with the apnea monitor's readout.

Diane Spencer offered a chilling explanation as to why she murdered three of her children: she just felt like she wanted to kill them. She insisted that she loved them but at the same time felt a need to destroy them.

At one point, Spencer asked, "What is going to happen to me?" and then answered her own question. "It doesn't matter. I'll go to prison and get killed there."[240] Child killers, she perhaps realized, did not fare well in the Big House.

The shocking admissions led to a first-degree murder charge and a possible life sentence without the possibility of parole.

While Diane Spencer contemplated the specter of life in a Michigan prison, Pennsylvania authorities began to build a case that could end with a lethal injection. A few days after Diane's shocking admissions, Clearfield County coroner Joel Heath requested an exhumation of Joyce Denochick.

Spencer attempted to block the exhumation by writing a letter to the court.

"Records will show Joyce Anne was on life support for several days before her death," she wrote. "Before determining to stop life support I was informed that her inner organs were deteriorating, there was minimal brain activity that added to normal body decomposition."[241]

Spencer's admissions were louder than her protests, and the court allowed the exhumation. A subsequent autopsy, coupled with Spencer's confession, led to the conclusion that the infant had died of asphyxiation from smothering. The death certificates for both Joyce and Autumn were subsequently changed with "asphyxiation" listed as the cause of death.

Three days before Spencer's murder trial commenced in Michigan, she was charged with two counts of murder in Pennsylvania.

After a period of psychiatric testing, Spencer's trial took place at the end of January 1992. On the third day, she took the stand in her own defense and attempted to retract, or at least recast, her confession of smothering her son.

She had woken up at about 4:00 a.m. and removed the baby monitor. She fed Aaron and then fell asleep with him on the couch, only to wake up and find him not breathing. "I picked Aaron up," she said. "He didn't respond with a gasp of air.…I breathed for Aaron a couple times and tried to find a pulse.…I realized at that point the monitor was not on. I hit the monitor, I don't know how many times, a couple of times, trying to find the pulse that I was trying to find with my hand, and it kept alarming. I was in a panic."[242]

It was a convenient explanation to counter the powerful evidence of the monitor readout.

She characterized her confession as the result of a guilty conscience over failing to save Aaron. It was that guilt that pushed her into confessing to a crime she did not commit.

When I did CPR on my son, he died. To a degree, at that point, I felt responsible…I did not know what to think anymore. I did not—I know what I felt, and what I believed, and that is that I love Aaron very much, and that intentionally, or unintentionally, or at any other way, that I would not have taken my son's life. My son was my life. But, the more that it went on, and the more accusations that were made, and the more I was relapsing, and failing, and screwing everything up, I thought, well maybe. Maybe they are right.[243]

The jury did not accept Spencer's ex post facto explanation. After deliberating for four hours, they voted to convict, which came with a mandatory life sentence.

Following the Michigan trial, Pennsylvania authorities moved for Spencer's extradition and prepared to try her for the murders of her two daughters. This time, a conviction could mean a possible death sentence.

In the end, Diane Spencer was saved by a technicality. The case fell apart when a Pennsylvania court ruled that Spencer's statements about Joyce and Autumn were inadmissible. For a confession to be admissible under Pennsylvania law at the time, law enforcement officers were required to inform a suspect about what they intended to ask and re-mirandize the suspect before questioning about separate crimes. Michigan law did not require officers to follow these strictures. Although Spencer signed a waiver and agreed to proceed without a defense attorney present, her confession did not meet the Pennsylvania criteria. Without the confessions, prosecutors had no case.

Diane Spencer, no. 222981, is serving life without the possibility of parole in the Women's Huron Valley Correctional Facility.

NOTES

1. Rogue's Gallery

1. *Detroit Free Press*, June 26, 1866; November 21, 1866.
2. *Detroit Free Press*, February 24, 1883; July 13, 1883.
3. *People of the State of Michigan v. Rosa Schweistahl*.
4. *Allegan Journal*, June 7, 1869.
5. *Allegan Journal*, August 9, 1869.
6. *Evening Leader*, April 22; July 12, 1879; *Weekly Leader*, May 3, 1882.
7. *Saginaw Weekly Courier*, January 4, 1877; *Saginaw Courier-Herald*, October 24, 1882.
8. *Saginaw Weekly Courier*, January 4, 1877; *Saginaw Courier-Herald*, August 12, 1880; October 24, 1882; July 29, 1886.
9. *Lake County Star*, February 17, 1881.
10. *Belding Banner-News*, January 22, 1919.
11. *Muskegon Chronicle*, December 30, 1886.
12. *Livingston Republican*, November 13, 1907.
13. *Detroit Free Press*, May 20, 1895; June 5, 1895; *Detroit Times*, January 1, 1917.
14. *Evening News*, December 20, 1899; *Grand Rapids Herald*, December 21, 1899; *Detroit Free Press*, October 6, 1903.
15. *Alma Record*, November 29, 1901.
16. *Evening Press*, February 15, 1902.
17. *Owosso Times*, December 18, 1903.
18. *Daily Herald*, January 5, 1905; *Detroit Free Press*, February 18, 1905.

19. *Detroit Free Press*, November 12, 1961; *Lansing State Journal*, April 26, 1962.
20. *Lansing State Journal*, December 10, 12, 1912; March 30–April 9, 1913; January 1, 1921.
21. *Muskegon Chronicle*, May 20–22, 1915; January 4, 1927.
22. *Detroit Free Press*, March 31, 1915; April 12, 1915; December 11, 1924. *Detroit Times*, March 25–31, 1915; December 24, 1924.
23. *Belding Banner News*, October 2, 16, 1918.
24. *Isabella County Enterprise*, April 18, 25, 1919; May 2, 1919.
25. *Leelanau Enterprise*, November 13, 27, 1919.
26. *Saginaw Daily News*, June 20–30, 1920; January 12–24, 1921; October 12, 1934.
27. *Detroit Free Press*, June 15, 1921; December 11, 1932; September 17, 1940.
28. *News-Palladium*, October 25, 1922.
29. *Battle Creek Enquirer*, November 22, 1922; *Lansing State Journal*, May 21, 1926.
30. *Detroit Free Press*, September 25, 1920; *Ludington Daily News*, October 5–7, 1920.
31. *Detroit Times*, October 26, 1949; *Lansing State Journal*, October 30, 1949.
32. *Battle Creek Enquirer*, April 18–19, 1923; October 16–18, 1923; *Jackson Citizen Patriot*, October 16–18, 1923; May 11, 1926. Kuhn's personal history from *Jackson News*, April 6, 1923.
33. *Lansing State Journal*, May 24, 1923; January 8, 1945; January 17, 1945.
34. *Detroit Free Press*, May 16, 1924; April 10, 1936.
35. *Detroit Free Press*, December 13, 1924; August 29, 1961.
36. *Detroit Free Press*, June 30, 1924; April 25, 1936; *Detroit Times*, December 23, 1936.

2. A Day in the Life

37. *Detroit News-Tribune*, July 16, 1899.
38. *Detroit Free Press*, January 12, 1890.
39. Ibid.
40. *Detroit Free Press*, January 12, 1890.
41. The pages containing the female inmates can be found in 1900 U.S. Census, Ward Seven in the City of Detroit, Wayne County, Michigan, Enumeration District 209, Sheets 5A and 5B, NARA Microfilm publication T623, National Archives and Records Administration, Washington, D.C.
42. *Detroit Free Press*, October 22, 1898.
43. *Detroit Free Press*, July 30, 1899.
44. *Detroit Free Press*, March 21, 1899.

45. *Detroit Free Press*, September 16, 1898.

46. *Detroit Free Press*, April 9, 1899.

47. *Detroit Free Press*, March 15, 1899.

48. The *Free Press* did an exposé of the "woman's corridor" that appeared in the April 9, 1899 edition. Asked about carrying a weapon, Brainard responded, "No we do not go armed; we have such good discipline that it [is] not necessary."

3. Taken for a Ride

49. *Herald-Press*, August 13, 1924. The note said, "I am sorry that I wasn't home last night as you came over. But I will tell you what I will do. You come down to St. Joseph Wednesday and I will meet you at Knaack's Drug store at 8 o'clock fast time, and we will be married. I will get the license before Wednesday you see. I left my farm and am working in St. Joe. I can't lay off or will lose my job. Now if you want to get married Wednesday night meet me at Knaack's Drug store at 8 o'clock fast time."

50. *Herald-Press*, August 15, 1924.

51. Ibid.

52. *Detroit Free Press*, August 24, 1924.

53. *Herald-Press*, August 15, 1924.

54. *Herald-Press*, August 14, 1924; August 16, 1924. Gore must have suspected that Zupke hit Raber. "Did you hit her?" he asked. Following Zupke's denial, he asked, "Did you slug her in any way?"

55. In place of a specific cause of death, the death certificate—signed by the country coroner on August 15, 1924—contains the notation "Murdered. Investigation still pending." Cora Raber Death Certificate, August 15, 1924, Royalton Township, Berrien County, Michigan Department of Health, Division of Vital Statistics, Lansing, Michigan.

56. *Herald-Press*, August 13, 1924.

57. *Herald-Press*, August 14, 1924.

58. "Did Florence McKinney Plan Cora Raber's Death?" *Detroit Free Press*, August 24, 1924.

59. When questioning Zupke at the preliminary hearing, Berrien County prosecutor Gore asked him about the conversation between Raber and Zupke before Zupke drove to McKinney's house. "Was Cora Raber alive then?" he asked. After Zupke responded with "Yes," Gore retorted, "Sure about that?" Gore later asked Zupke if Raber was alive or dead when

they arrived at the McKinney residence. When Zupke responded with "Alive," Gore again asked, "Sure about that?" This line of questioning was possibly motivated by Zupke's first confession, in which he attempted to shield Florence McKinney by claiming that he killed Cora Raber *before* he went to the McKinney residence. The *Herald-Press* printed a Q & A transcript of Zupke's testimony in the August 22, 1924 edition.

60. *Herald-Press*, August 13, 1924.
61. Zupke gave his first confession on Tuesday, August 12. He made a second confession to the court stenographer on Thursday, August 14. Both the *News-Palladium* and the *Herald-Press* printed the verbatim confession in Q & A format in their Saturday, August 16, 1924 editions.
62. *Herald-Press*, August 16, 1924.
63. Ibid.
64. Ibid.
65. Ibid.
66. *Herald-Press*, August 15, 1924.
67. *Herald-Press*, August 16, 1924.
68. Ibid.
69. *Herald-Press*, August 22, 1924.
70. *News-Palladium*, December 4, 1924.
71. Ibid.
72. *Lansing State Journal*, November 21, 1935.
73. *News-Palladium*, January 6, 1973.

4. For Services Rendered

74. *Herald-Press*, June 5–6, 1928.
75. Cook's death certificate lists cause of death as "Gunshot wound inflicted by 38 cal. Revolver fired by Margaret [sic] Bumbaugh." Death Record for Cook, Walter H., March 30, 1928, Michigan Department of Health, Disease Control, Record and Statistics Division, Death Records, 1928, Berrien County, 005363558_02538.
76. *News-Palladium*, March 31, 1928.
77. With the advent of suffrage in 1920, women were legally entitled to serve on juries. By the time of the Bumbaugh trial in 1928, the woman juror was no longer a rarity, but the court often did not assign female jurors to murder trials to spare them lengthy absences from what was assumed to be their domestic responsibilities. According to a front-page article in

the *Herald-Press* of June 5, 1928, all of the jurors were married men with children, which may have benefitted Bumbaugh's defense.

78. *Herald-Press* published both poems in the April 11, 1928 edition.

79. *Herald-Press*, June 6, 1928.

80. Ibid.

81. *News-Palladium*, June 7, 1928.

82. *Herald-Press*, June 8, 1928.

83. 1930 US Census, "Marguerite Bumbaugh," Ward 7 in the City of Detroit, in the County of Wayne, Michigan, enumeration district 182, sheet 3A, line 12, NARA microfilm publication T626, roll 1038, National Archives and Records Administration, Washington, D.C. Sources disagree about Bumbaugh's age. According to an account of the trial in the *News-Palladium* of June 7, 1928, this confusion stemmed from her booking at the county jail, when she gave her age as thirty-two. In court, Bumbaugh stated her age as thirty-one, and the 1930 U.S. Census, which lists her age as thirty-two, verifies this assertion. At the time the census takers visited, she was incarcerated in the Detroit House of Correction, where she served her sentence alongside lifers Minera Abass, Louise McKnight and Ethel Walker (see "Rogue's Gallery").

84. This portion of Bumbaugh's testimony from the *Herald-Press* of June 8, 1928. Both the *Herald-Press* and the *News-Palladium* quoted lengthy sections of Deetie's testimony, but the wording differs slightly between the two accounts.

85. None of the news accounts disclose the nature of this "business," but it is possible that Cook had contracted syphilis at some point and gave it to Deetie rather than the other way around. Answering Donahue's query, she insisted that she had never had an affair with any man other than Cook. Cook, on the other hand, according to Deetie, bragged of his other affairs.

86. This portion of Bumbaugh's testimony from the *News-Palladium*, June 8, 1928.

87. Quoted in the *News-Palladium*, June 8, 1928.

88. *News-Palladium*, June 8, 1928.

89. The *Herald Press* of June 8, 1928, contained four pages devoted to the trial.

90. The *Herald-Press* of June 8, 1928, published both poems.

5. The "Baby Murder Farm" Case

91.. *Herald-Press*, February 13, 1929.

92. *News-Palladium*, February 14, 1929.

93. Ibid.

94. Clarence Wesley Gorham Death Certificate, February 10, 1929, Village of Eau Claire, Berrien County, Michigan Department of Health, Division of Vital Statistics, Lansing, Michigan.

95. Louise May Gorham Death Certificate, February 21, 1923, Silver Creek Township, Cass County, Michigan Department of Health, Division of Vital Statistics, Lansing, Michigan.

96. Mary Jane Gorham Death Certificate, March 1, 1925, Dowagiac, Cass County, Michigan, Department of Health, Division of Vital Statistics, Lansing, Michigan.

97. Isabelle May Gorham Death Certificate, May 25, 1925, Village of Eau Claire, Berrien County, Michigan Department of Health, Division of Vital Statistics, Lansing, Michigan.

98. A *News-Palladium* reporter's interview with Herbert was published in the February 14, 1949 edition.

99. *News-Palladium*, February 13, 1949.

100. In the Wednesday, February 13, 1929 edition, the *News-Palladium* published a Q & A transcript of Oakel Gorham's statement.

101. *Herald Press*, February 13, 1929.

102. Ibid.

103. *Herald Press*, February 14, 1929.

104. *News-Palladium*, February 13, 1929; *Herald Press*, February 13, 1929. Both news accounts contain this statement without variation.

105. *News-Palladium*, February 14, 1929; *Herald Press*, February 14, 1929.

106. *News-Palladium*, February 14, 1929.

107. *News-Palladium*, February 13, 1929.

108. *News-Palladium*, February 15, 1929.

109. *News-Palladium*, February 14, 1929.

110. *Herald Press*, February 14, 1929.

111. The *Herald Press* edition of February 14, 1919, discussed the new law. "An administration sterilization bill—designed to prevent recurrence of such crimes as the St. Joseph case in which a feeble-minded mother admitted participation in the murder of six or more children will be introduced within a few days, Governor Fred W. Green said today." The "St. Joseph case" is an oblique reference to the Eau Claire "Murder Farm."

112. *News-Palladium*, February 14, 1929.

113. *News-Palladium*, February 20, 1929.

114. *Detroit Free Press*, Sunday, March 3, 1929.

115. Excerpts of the report published in the *News-Palladium*, March 9, 1929.

116. *News-Palladium*, November 26, 1956.

6. The Heiress and the Mechanic

117. 1920 U.S. Census, Ward One in the City of Chicago, Cook County, Illinois, Enumeration District 30, Sheet 1A, House 215, NARA Microfilm publication T625, National Archives and Records Administration, Washington, D.C.; 1930 US Census, Ward Five in the City of Flint, Genesee County, Michigan, Enumeration District 42, Sheet 5B, House 521, NARA Microfilm publication T 626, National Archives and Records Administration, Washington, D.C.; 1940 US Census, Northville Township, Wayne County, Michigan, Enumeration District 82-195, Sheet 3A, Line 25, Detroit House of Correction, Women's Division, NARA Microfilm publication T627, National Archives and Records Administration, Washington, D.C. Sources disagree as to Helen Joy Morgan's age. Contemporary news articles published at the time of her trial state her age as twenty-six, but the U.S. Census of 1920 states her age at twenty-six and the U.S. Census of 1930 states her age at forty, making her forty-two in 1932. The 1940 Census, taken when Morgan was in the Detroit House of Correction, states her age at forty-eight, making her forty in 1932.
118. Testimony of Minnie Spiker quoted in the *Flint Daily Journal*, January 7, 1932.
119. *Flint Daily Journal*, January 8, 1932.
120. Testimony of Helen Hess née Singer quoted in the *Flint Daily Journal*, January 7, 1932.
121. *Flint Daily Journal*, second extra, April 25, 1931.
122. A series of articles detailing the Helen Joy Morgan murder trial, including transcripts of testimony, appeared in the *Flint Daily Journal*. Gray's testimony was published in the January 7, 1932 edition. The transcripts offered by the newspaper present a detailed and fairly complete record of proceedings at the trial. The testimony is presented in Q & A format, which preserves the back-and-forth flow of a typical courtroom exchange between lawyers and witnesses. Some newspapers of the era condensed several answers into composite statements that were used to create narratives. Unlike the Q & A format, these narratives often give a misleading sense of the actual courtroom proceedings.
123. *Flint Daily Journal*, second extra, April 25, 1931.
124. Testimony of Homer L. Halstead quoted in the *Flint Daily Journal*, January 8, 1932.
125. Closing argument of John H. Farley quoted in the *Flint Daily Journal*, January 8, 1932.

126. Quoted in the *Flint Daily Journal*, January 14, 1932.

127. Quoted in the *Flint Daily Journal*, January 8, 1932.

128. The jury consisted of fourteen men, which included two alternates in case something happened to one of the other jurors. The alternates listened to testimony but were dismissed prior to deliberations.

129. Quoted in the *Flint Daily Journal*, January 14, 1932.

130. Quoted in the *Flint Daily Journal*, January 8, 1932.

131. Carrie P. Morgan, Death Certificate, Register No. 1088, Lansing, Michigan: Michigan Department of Health, Division of Vital Statistics, September 6, 1934.

7. All in the Family

132. 1930 US Census, "Darius Lambert," Aloha Township in the County of Cheboygan, Michigan, enumeration district 16-1, sheet 3A, dwelling 46, family 49, line 17, NARA microfilm publication T626, roll 1038, National Archives and Records Administration, Washington, D.C.; 1930 US Census, "Albert Lambert," Grant Township in the County of Cheboygan, Michigan, enumeration district 16-12, sheet 1B, dwelling 9, family 9, line 55, NARA microfilm publication T626, roll 1038, National Archives and Records Administration, Washington, D.C. Some reports spell his name "Dorias." In the 1930 U.S. Census, his name is spelled "Darius," so that is the name used throughout this chapter.

133. *Cheboygan Daily Tribune*, August 4, 1932.

134. The August 4, 1932 edition of the *Cheboygan Daily Tribune* summarizes testimony given at the coroner's inquest.

135. Albert said that he deliberately fired into the air to scare his brother. Afraid Darius saw him, he then decided he had little choice but to kill him. It is more likely that Albert changed his mind at the last second or simply missed the first shot.

136. A partial transcript of Albert's confession, presented in Q & A format, appeared in the August 8, 1932 edition of the *Cheboygan Daily Tribune*.

137. According to Albert, Minnie first approached him about killing Darius in the spring, which is most likely when she discovered she was pregnant. Fears of concealing her pregnancy would also explain why she nagged Albert to shoot his brother.

138. *Cheboygan Daily Tribune*, August 8, 1932.

139. Albert Lambert, Certificate of Death, August 29, 1944, Michigan Department of Health, Bureau of Records and Statistics, Lansing, Michigan .

8. Chemical Divorce

140. 1900 US Census, Township of Bearinger, County of Presque Isle, State of Michigan, Enumeration District 153, Sheet 1A, Dwelling 1, Schedule No. 1—Population, Indian Population, NARA microfilm publication T623, National Archives and Record Administration, Washington, D.C. The census record indicates that "Lizzie Moreau" emigrated in 1890 and describes her nativity as one-half Chippewa. Her birthdate is listed as January 1875 and her age as twenty-five. The record also indicates that in 1900, she had been married for ten years, which put her marriage in 1890—the same year she moved to Michigan—when Lizzie was fifteen years old. Curiously, the record states that she could write but not read.

141. *L'Anse Sentinel*, January 5, 1933. John Boston died on March 10, 1932. According to an article published in the *L'Anse Sentinel*, Elizabeth married John Ziolokowski the following October 17.

142. *L'Anse Sentinel*, October 13, 1932.

143. Quoted in the *Escanaba Daily Press*, January 4, 1933.

144. *L'Anse Sentinel*, January 5, 1933.

145. Quoted in the *Detroit Free Press*, February 24, 1961.

146. Quoted in the *Detroit Free Press*, 24, 1961.

9. Three Sirens

147. *Detroit Free Press*, July 2, 1935. "Talk of the Yawkey millions led Howard Carter Dickinson to his death. That is the police theory in the strangest crime ever to be committed in Detroit, rattling as it has the skeletons in one of Michigan's wealthiest and oldest families."

148. *Detroit Times*, June 28, 1935. The birth certificate listed Sadie Harper and Raymond Mills as the parents.

149. *Detroit Free Press*, July 2, 1935.

150. *Detroit Free Press*, June 28, 1935.

151. *Detroit Times*, June 28, 1935.

152. *Detroit Free Press*, June 29, 1935. The wording of Smygen's account in the *Free Press* varies slightly from the wording presented in the *Times*, although the content and context remains the same.

153. *Detroit Free Press*, June 29, 1935.

154. Ibid.

155. *Detroit Times*, June 28, 1935.

156. *Detroit Free Press*, June 30, 1935.

157. *Detroit Free Press*, July 1, 1935.

158. *Detroit Times*, July 2, 1935.

159. *Detroit Free Press*, July 2, 1935.

160. The *Detroit Times* of June 30, 1935, contained an exclusive interview with Anna Jackson.

161. *Detroit Times*, July 28, 1935.

162. *Detroit Free Press*, July 2, 1935.

163. *Detroit Free Press*, August 3, 1935.

164. *Detroit Free Press*, July 1, 1935.

165. *Detroit Free Press*, July 2, 1935. Investigators questioned the three women together. After they escorted the Jackson sisters back to their cells, they interviewed Jean Miller. For the first time, she broke their conspiracy of silence and admitted that the robbery was planned (although she said she knew nothing about the murder ahead of time). The Jackson sisters followed suit and revised their earlier statements.

166. *Detroit Free Press*, July 2, 1935.

167. Ibid.

168. Ibid.

169. *Detroit Free Press*, July 2, 1935. Jean Miller's statement contained the following: "I remember Bill saying before we started out, 'If we're lucky and get at least a thousand dollars we'll get a tent and put on our own shows.' You know we girls had been trying to break into the show game and make a living that way."

170. *Detroit Times*, July 28, 1935.

171. *Detroit Free Press*, August 6, 1935.

172. *Detroit Free Press*, August 16, 1935.

173. *Detroit Free Press*, November 27, 1948.

174. Patrick S. McDougall, "Murder of a Big Shot," in Hamer, *Detroit Murders*, 154.

10. You Belong to Me: Murder of the Love Slave

175. *Detroit Times*, January 10, 1937.
176. *Detroit Times*, January 10, 1937. Sources differ about how and when Betty met Schneider. This version is from her testimony at the trial and quoted in the January 8, 1937 edition of the *Detroit Free Press*. Albert Baker testified that he introduced Betty to Schneider when he invited the bowling team to his residence.
177. *Detroit Free Press*, January 10, 1937.
178. *Detroit Times*, January 5, 1937.
179. *Detroit Free Press*, January 7, 1937.
180. Ibid.
181. *Detroit Times*, January 10, 1937.
182. Ibid.; *Detroit Free Press*, January 9, 1937.
183. *Detroit Free Press*, January 8, 1937.
184. *Detroit Free Press*, January 9, 1937.
185. *Detroit Free Press*, January 14, 1937.
186. *Detroit Times*, January 12, 1937.
187. *Detroit Free Press*, January 13, 1937.
188. *Detroit Free Press*, January 14, 1937.
189. *Detroit Free Press*, January 15, 1937.

11. Housden, We Have a Problem

190. *Detroit Free Press*, April 26, 1945.
191. 1940 US Census, "Nina Perkins," magisterial district 2, in the County of Morgan, Kentucky, enumeration district 88-10, family 146, sheet 9A, line 2, NARA microfilm publication T627, roll 1343, National Archives and Records Administration, Washington, D.C.; 1930 US Census, "Nina Debard," magisterial district 2, in the County of Morgan, Kentucky, enumeration district 88-10, family 111, sheet 6, line 98, NARA microfilm publication T626, roll 771, National Archives and Records Administration, Washington, D.C. Contemporary news reports state that Nina was thirty-two in 1944, but census records indicate she was twenty-nine.
192. *Detroit Free Press*, April 25, 1945. Nina testified that her first husband agreed to a divorce because they were unable to have children.
193. *Detroit Times*, December 26, 1944.
194. *Detroit Free Press*, December 25, 1944.

195. *Detroit Free Press*, December 26, 1944.
196. Ibid.
197. Ibid.
198. *Detroit Times*, April 25, 1945.
199. *Detroit Times*, April 28, 1945.
200. *Detroit Times*, April 26, 1945.
201. *Detroit Evening Times*, April 27, 1945.
202. *Detroit Free Press*, April 26, 1945.

12. The Housewife and the Orphan

203. *Lansing State Journal*, September 7, 1947. "The two boys and Mrs. Upton watched Upton die, according to [Ingham County Prosecutor Charles] MacLean."
204. *Lansing State Journal*, September 6, 1947.
205. *Lansing State Journal*, January 13, 1948.
206. *Lansing State Journal*, September 7, 1947.
207. Ibid.
208. Ibid.
209. *Lansing State Journal*, September 6, 1947.
210. *Lansing State Journal*, September 12, 1947. At the murder trial, state police captain Lawrence Meehan testified to asking Richard about the nature of his relationship with Josephine Upton. "I asked him how intimate he and Josephine had been," Meehan testified, "and he said they had not been intimate. He said she had kissed him once on the nape of the neck."
211. *Lansing State Journal*, December 20, 1948. At the trial, Josephine adamantly denied using chain-smoking to kill her appetite when Prosecutor Charles MacLean asked, "Isn't it a fact, you smoked one cigarette after another to keep you from having an appetite?"
212. *Lansing State Journal*, September 7, 1947.
213. *Lansing State Journal*, December 17, 1947.
214. *Lansing State Journal*, December 19, 1947.
215. Ibid.
216. *Lansing State Journal*, December 23, 1947.
217. *Lansing State Journal*, January 13, 1947.

13. The Bark Is Worse Than the Bite

218. *People of the State of Michigan v. Carol Ege*, No. 173448, (August 25, 2009), 7.
219. *People of the State of Michigan v. Carol Ege*, No. 173448 (September 17, 1996), 3; (August 25, 2009), 4.
220. *Detroit Free Press*, July 28, 2005.
221. *People of the State of Michigan v. Carol Ege*, No. 173448 (September 17, 1996), 3.
222. Ibid., 22.
223. Ibid., 24.
224. Ibid.
225. *Detroit Free Press*, July 28, 2005.
226. *Lansing State Journal*, November 29, 2007.
227. *People of the State of Michigan v. Carol Ege*, No. 173448 (August 25, 2009), 9.
228. Ibid., 18–19.

14. Twisted Fairy Tale

229. Quoted in the *Detroit Free Press*, January 18, 1995.
230. Quoted in the *Detroit Free Press*, Oakland Final, October 23, 1998.
231. *People of the State of Michigan v. Debra Lynn Starr* in the Oakland County Circuit Court, State of Michigan Court of Appeals Opinion (unpublished), March 16, 2001, 3.

15. Bad Things Happen in Threes

232. *Detroit News*, December 13, 1990. During her stay at a rehabilitation center following Aaron's death, Spencer penned a twelve-page autobiographical piece, portions of which were printed in newspapers in December 1990.
233. Testimony of Diane Louise Spencer, January 29, 1992. *People of the State of Michigan v. Diane Louise Spencer*, Volume III, File No. 91-8787-FH, 134; *Grand Rapids Press*, January 29, 1992.
234. *Detroit News*, December 12, 1990; *Pittsburgh Press*, January 6, 1991.
235. *Detroit News*, December 13, 1990.
236. *Times-Leader*, October 29, 1992.
237. See note 232. Quoted in the *Detroit News*, December 13, 1990.

238. For a thorough discussion of the forensic evidence, see Buhk and Cohle, *Skeletons in the Closet*.
239. Testimony of Diane Louise Spencer, 132.
240. Quoted in the *Grand Rapids Press*, January 29, 1992.
241. Quoted in the *Centre Daily Times*, December 28, 1990.
242. Testimony of Diane Louise Spencer, 128.
243. Ibid., 136–37.

BIBILIOGRAPHY

Newspapers

Papers are from Michigan unless otherwise stated.

Allegan Journal
Alma Record
Battle Creek Enquirer
Belding Banner-News
Centre Daily Times (State College, PA)
Cheboygan Daily Tribune
Daily Herald (Port Huron)
Detroit Evening-Times
Detroit Free Press
Detroit News
Detroit News-Tribune
Detroit Times
Evening Leader (Grand Rapids)
Evening News (Grand Rapids)
Flint Daily Journal
Grand Rapids Herald
Grand Rapids Press
Herald-Press (St. Joseph)
Isabella County Enterprise

Jackson Citizen Patriot
Jackson News
Lake County Star (Chase)
L'Anse Sentinel (Baraga)
Lansing State Journal
Leelanau Enterprise
Livingston Republican
Ludington Daily News
Muskegon Chronicle
News-Palladium (Benton Harbor)
Owosso Times
Pittsburgh (PA) Press
Saginaw Courier-Herald
Saginaw Daily News
Saginaw Weekly Courier
Times-Leader (Wilkes-Barre, PA)
Weekly Leader (Grand Rapids)

Books, Articles, Documents and Archives

Buhk, Tobin T. "Life Behind Bars: The Women of the Detroit House of Correction." *Michigan History Magazine* 101, no. 5 (September–October 2017).
———. "The Most Dangerous Women in Michigan's History." *Michigan History Magazine* 103, no. 2 (March–April 2019).
Buhk, Tobin T., and Stephen D. Cohle. *Skeletons in the Closet: Stories from the County Morgue.* New York: Prometheus Books, 2008.
Federal Censuses of 1900, 1910, 1920, 1930, 1940.
Hamer, Alvin C., ed. *Detroit Murders.* New York: Duell, Sloan and Pearce, 1948.
Michigan Department of Health, Record and Statistics Division, Death Records. Digital images available at michiganology.org.
People of the State of Michigan v. Caroline Collins. State of Michigan Supreme Court.
People of the State of Michigan v. Carol Ege. State of Michigan Court of Appeals Opinion (unpublished), September 17, 1996.
People of the State of Michigan v. Carol Ege. State of Michigan Court of Appeals Opinion (unpublished), August 25, 2009.
People of the State of Michigan v. Rosa Schweistahl. Recorder's Court for the City of Detroit, State of Michigan, County of Wayne, case file 1295, Archives of Michigan.

People of the State of Michigan v. Diane Louise Spencer. Volume III, File No. 91-8787-FH.

People of the State of Michigan v. Debra Lynn Starr. Oakland County Circuit Court, State of Michigan Court of Appeals Opinion (unpublished), March 16, 2001.

ABOUT THE AUTHOR

A connoisseur of crime, a gourmet of the ghastly, an aficionado of the atrocious, a fanatic of the felonious and a maven of misdeeds, author and researcher Tobin T. Buhk enjoys exploring the back alleys of Michigan history and shining a light on the contemptible characters and dastardly deeds hiding in its darkest corners. To research his first book, he spent a year as a volunteer at the Kent County Morgue. Find his speaking schedule at www.tobinbuhk.com or take a walk on the dark side of history at his blog, www.darkcornersofhistory.com.

Visit us at
www.historypress.com
···